THE GOOD PLACE

THE URBAN DESIGN GROUP, whose members provided a great deal of background information for *The Good Place Guide* and were involved in many of the featured projects, was founded in 1978 because there was a wide difference of views in the professions about the way to achieve quality in the places where we live and work. Its objectives were to provide a forum for those who believed that planning should be more concerned with the quality of places and to encourage all the professions to be involved. It was clear that everyone with an interest in their surroundings had a part to play whether they were professionals, developers, councillors or members of affected communities.

Making successful places depends on breaking down professional barriers, on building collaborations between the people who can make things happen, and on making sure that all involved have the necessary skills and understanding.

The Urban Design Group has a wide membership and organises lectures, conferences, regional events and study tours, and publishes *Urban Design Quarterly* and *The Urban Design Source Book*. Membership details can be obtained from its office at 70 Cowcross Street, London EC1M 6DG; telephone 020 7250 0892; fax 020 7250 0872; e-mail admin@udg.org.uk.

THE GOOD PLACE GUIDE

URBAN DESIGN IN BRITAIN AND IRELAND
/ JOHN BILLINGHAM AND RICHARD COLE

BATSFORD

BRITISH LIBRARY CATALOGUING IN PUBLICATION
A CIP RECORD FOR THIS BOOK IS AVAILABLE FROM THE BRITISH LIBRARY

PUBLISHED BY B T BATSFORD, A member of **Chrysalis** Books plc
64 BREWERY ROAD, LONDON N7 9NT
WWW.BATSFORD.COM
SERIES EDITOR TOM NEVILLE
SERIES DESIGN CLAUDIA SCHENK

FIRST PUBLISHED 2002
COPYRIGHT © URBAN DESIGN GROUP 2002

ISBN 0 7134 8786 0

PRINTED IN SPAIN BY JUST COLOUR GRAPHIC, S.L.

FOR A COPY OF THE BATSFORD CATALOGUE OR INFORMATION
ON SPECIAL QUANTITY ORDERS OF BATSFORD BOOKS PLEASE
CONTACT US ON 020 7697 3000 OR SALES@CHRYSALISBOOKS.CO.UK

John Billingham and Richard Cole

CONTENTS

INTRODUCTION 0

USING THE GUIDE 0.22

LONDON 1

SOUTH EAST ENGLAND 2

EASTERN ENGLAND 3

SOUTHERN ENGLAND 4

SOUTH-WEST ENGLAND AND SOUTH WALES 5

THE MIDLANDS 6

NORTH-WEST ENGLAND AND NORTH WALES 7

NORTHERN ENGLAND 8

SCOTLAND 9

IRELAND 10

INDEX 11

FOREWORD
JOHN WORTHINGTON

In 1989 when I was invited to be president of the Urban Design Group, one of the initiatives I launched was the idea of a good place guide, to be compiled from the experiences of members of the group and invited contributions. Hope has finally become reality, largely due to the dedication and perseverance of John Billingham and Richard Cole.

The idea of the guide was inspired by Egon Ronay's *Good Food Guide* which recognised the central importance of imaginatively chosen menus, impeccably prepared from well-sourced ingredients. But entries were chosen not merely for gastronomic excellence but also for the experience of the meal. Good places, I felt, had similar qualities. While architects and their builders could create good spaces, it was people and interaction that created memorable places; it is that interaction of vernacular building, the gradual growth of custom and the experience of the community that has made the places we enjoy and respect today. Enjoyable places are also very personal. When reflecting on places for this guide, contributions were as much about memories of an event in a place or a feeling of well-being as they were about pure formal space, or material character. When we were first establishing the character and boundaries of the guide, my immediate choice of a good place was Waterloo Bridge. Some feel that a bridge is a non-place. Architecturally, it does not contain space, but merely delineates space. It is a through-way, rather than a point of rest, not one well-defined space, but a set of experiences. My argument for Waterloo Bridge is that it is a distinctive place for many people, for the very reason that it can be experienced in so many different ways, and encompasses such a rich collection of memories: the 'river of fire' on Millennium night; parking on the bridge and walking back to the National Theatre; frantic taxi rides to catch the Eurostar; that memorable glimpse of St Paul's dome to one side and Big Ben to the other, lit up in the gathering gloom.

One of my favourite examples of non-designed space, which encapsulates the essence of its location, is Mill Lane Bridge, Cambridge. The edges and viewpoints of such a place are blurred. It can be entered either from the confines of Mill Lane, defined by high college walls to one side and University buildings to the other, or through a meadow landscape along the river. The place itself is a combination of the bridge, the punt landing, the footpath in front of the pub, and the mill pond. It is a melting pot of gown, town and visitor, punctuated by the recent architectural addition of Dixon Jones' study bedrooms for Downing College, across the mill pond, and Howell Killick and Partridge's University Centre. Memories encompass May Ball evening, a relaxed drink after a meeting with the University administration, or the calm of lying in the meadow.

The impact of increased mobility and the access to ideas and information afforded by information technology have fundamentally changed the way we perceive the city. Our sense of community is less about the simple geographical place we inhabit, but perhaps more about our community of interest. My community can stretch from San Francisco to Venice, linked by the web and cheap travel. With greater mobility, the location we choose in our 'city of the mind' as our urban 'quarters' for learning, work or leisure, may be as much about its quality of place and service as its geographical location. The move to the virtual world afforded by telecommunications places even greater demands on the need for physical spaces that combine both form and meaning.

It is heartening to recognise that many of the examples of good places chosen for this publication are recently completed new-built projects (Broadgate and Tower Bridge Piazza in London, and Brindleyplace Square, Birmingham). Other examples are pedestrianisation schemes (Dundee and Buchanan Street, Glasgow), or urban-regeneration projects (Castlefield in Manchester, Temple Bar in Dublin), where the quality of experience has arisen from the organic mix of new and old and gradual accretion.

INTRODUCTION

We all remember places that we like and enjoy using or visiting. They may help us to recall happy times, they may be places that we visited as children, they may have historic connections or present a delightful combination of landscape and buildings. There is a wide range of locations that can be considered 'good places' and most of them could described as historic. They have been created over long periods of time and exist almost by accident. The small towns of the Cotswolds, the seaside villages of Devon, the villages that nestle at the foot of the South Downs, sometimes containing a small square, quaint streets or courtyards that intrigue, are examples of these accidental places. In reality, of course, they are not wholly accidental; they reflect the specific needs of the people who built them, the materials available locally and the form of the land upon which they were founded. They are almost organic in character. However, not all historic places have this organic origin – some are the result of deliberate design and are the product of what could be called a masterplan. Parts of Bath, Edinburgh's New Town and classical Dublin are examples of these planned places.

Very few new places seem to have the qualities of these historic precedents. Why is it that so few of the places we build now are places we like?

Change is rarely welcome: we enjoy the familiar and resent the loss of cherished symbols. This concern was one of the reasons that the 1947 Planning Act introduced a system under which all development was brought under control and required planning consent. At its crudest, this was negative control. It could prevent the worst but it could do little to encourage the good. Individual developers could act in their own interests and if thwarted through failure to get planning consent merely walk away to find another site and try again. While the Act was not entirely negative – local authorities had the power to define 'Comprehensive Development Areas' where a positive overview could be taken –

the procedures were cumbersome and time-consuming. Problems of local-authority finance and a desire to separate functions like housing from work or leisure meant that many of the designated areas became grim places where monolithic architecture and single-minded road systems seemed designed to alienate people.

In reaction, public opinion turned again to familiar historic places. The Civic Trust was established in 1957 with the aims of safeguarding valued places and enhancing them. While the Trust could only encourage and identify good examples, it struck a chord in the heart of some in Government and new legislation was created which introduced Conservation Areas. These could be designated to safeguard historic places but they did little to promote the quality of new development beyond the scale of a single building. We seemed to have lost the art of what had been called civic design. A few set-pieces, particularly university buildings, hinted that new places of quality could be created, but something was missing   developments with a single use created dull and uniform places. They lacked the buzz of older places. In some locations, like the new towns, each element performed its function well enough, but seemed isolated. What the author and designer Gordon Cullen called 'Townscape' was missing. To some practitioners the system of development control set up to safeguard the urban environment was actually setting architects against planners, landscape architects against engineers.

In 1978 an open meeting to address these concerns was called at the Royal Institute of British Architects. A steering committee was set up under Francis Tibbalds and the group which came to be called the Urban Design Group established. Its objective was to seek the improvement of the design of the physical environment and the quality of places and to encourage all the professions to combine to achieve this. It was recognised that everyone involved with the urban environment was an urban designer because it was their

INTRODUCTION

decisions that influenced the final quality of spaces. Urban design was defined as the 'art of making places for people'. It concerns the streets, squares and spaces that make up the public realm. The Urban Design Group subsequently identified four areas where progress was needed: a commitment from central government to take a greater interest in the design of the public realm; radical changes in the way the professions are educated to place urban design higher on the agenda; recognition by local authorities of the positive role that urban design can play; and finally that the community and the professions need to argue for better urban design which means added value for all users.

Progress has been made in all these areas. In 1994 central government published *Quality in Town and Country* which incorporated the vital role urban design can play in creating better-quality environments and included many of the objectives of the Urban Design Group. The idea of joined-up thinking involving all those contributing to the urban-design process was taken up by the main professional bodies concerned with the environment together with the Civic Trust and the Urban Design Group. In 1997 they combined to form the Urban Design Alliance. The government convened an Urban Task Force and in 1999 its report, *Towards an Urban Renaissance*, was published. This included a call for a national urban-design framework. The government also reviewed the role that the Royal Fine Arts Commission had played and in 1999 replaced this body with CABE – The Commission for Architecture and the Built Environment. Its remit is much broader and its design-review committees and *Project Framework* emphasise the need to understand the context of a scheme and make a positive contribution to the public realm. This was followed in 2000 by the publication by the government and CABE of *By Design – Urban design in the planning system: towards better practice*, and an *Urban Design Compendium* was published by English Partnerships and The Housing Corporation.

Urban design has clearly come of age. The bodies mentioned earlier consider it essential to promote the 'art of making places for people' and foster greater awareness of the objectives of urban design. This is one of the purposes of this *Good Place Guide*, for there is no escaping the results of urban design, good or bad. Only through experiencing the pleasure that can be derived from good design can we appreciate its value.

This book describes 128 places that people are likely to enjoy using or visiting. It concentrates on those places that have been created or significantly changed over the last 50 years and are good examples of the design of places as distinct from an individual building. It is based on earlier work produced by the Urban Design Group and it should be emphasised that it only covers part of the concerns of urban design. However, it demonstrates some of the key components of creating successful places through elements such as the mixture of uses, space for pedestrians and setting the design in its context.

The definition of 'a good place' is likely to be as elusive as the perfect good place itself. It needs to have 'a sense of place' and not, as Gertrude Stein put it when she went to Oakland in California, the sense that 'when you get there, there isn't any there there'. This sense of place needs to take into account these questions: is the place enjoyable – is it safe, human in scale, with a variety of uses?; is it environmentally friendly – sunlit, wind- and pollution-free?; is it memorable and identifiable – distinctive?; is it appropriate – does it relate to its context?; is access freely available?

Many places – such as Byker and Lillington Street, both of which are single-use – may not meet all the criteria. Some places where access is limited – such as the Victoria Quarter in Leeds and Portmeirion, which not only closes but charges for entry – have been included. Both of these were felt to be of such significance that it would be inappropriate to exclude them. This flexibility did not extend to the inclusion of the out-of-town shopping developments where their effect has been too damaging to surrounding areas, or where the character of a place depends almost totally on enclosed private space. The guide, however, includes places which meet most of the criteria. We have identified ten places which we think are the most successful examples: Broadgate and Covent Garden in London (pages 1.4 and 1.6); Brindleyplace Square in Birmingham (page 6.10); Portmeirion (page 7.24); Whitehaven's Waterfront (page 7.32); the Market Square, Hull (page 8.8); the Victoria Quarter, Leeds (page 8.14); East Quayside, Newcastle upon Tyne (page 8.18); Buchanan Street in Glasgow (page 9.10); and Dublin's Temple Bar (page 10.16).

It is almost inevitable that we have overlooked places that some consider significant. We apologise for any oversights and would be glad to learn of omissions. We can be contacted through the Urban Design Group at 70 Cowcross Street, London EC1M 6DG where details of membership can be obtained. The Group promotes urban design through lectures, seminars, conferences and study tours. It welcomes all people – not just professionals – who are interested in improving the urban environment.

Acknowledgements

The Good Place Guide has been produced over a number of years by the efforts of many individual members of the Urban Design Group and other people who are credited below. It could not have been achieved without their involvement nor without the forbearance of our wives, Pat and Lucy.

If this book were to be dedicated to people then the late Francis Tibbalds and Keith Ingham would be the most appropriate as they were two of the three people who initiated the idea of an Urban Design Group. Francis Tibbalds had an immense influence in putting urban design on to the public agenda and Keith Ingham was a key figure in the early days of working on a *Good Place Guide*. The Civic Trust was also very helpful in providing a number of images. Material from Ireland could not have been achieved without contributions provided by Pat and Gráinne Shaffrey and information from Margaret Coyle.

A distinguished panel assisted in producing a first trawl of almost 90 places for the guide which was subsequently increased to about 130 places. The panel consisted of Matthew Carmona, Roger Evans, Lora Nicolaou, Monica Pidgeon and Alan Stones.

Individual members and others who contributed to the guide included the following: Derek Abbott, John Biggs, James Brebner, Philip Cave, Sarah Collings, Michael Crilly, Richard Crutchley, Tony Dennis, Gerald Dix, Kevin Eastham, Brian Evans, Nicholas Falk, Sir Terry Farrell, Peter Fauset, Mike Galloway, Brian Goodey, Sir Peter Hall, Saskia Hallam, Peter Heath, Joe Holyoak, Bob Jarvis, Stefan Kruczkowski, Derek Latham, James Lenart, Sebastian Loew, Tom Longsdale, Colen Lumley, Rob McDonald, Chris Odgers, John Peverley, Rajesh Rana, Sam Romaya, Victor Rose, David Ross, Anthony Scott, Barry Sellers, Barry Shaw, Alan Stone, Mark Suppel, Bill Tavernor, Peter Taylor, John Templeton, Jane Tobin, Barrie Todd, Rob Warren, Jack Warshaw, Chris Wood and Geoff Wright.

A number of offices and local authorities provided information about places included in the guide: these included Birmingham City Council, Bolton Metropolitan Borough, Devon County Council, Dundee City Council, East Hertfordshire District Council, Horsham District Council, Gloucester City Council, Kingston-upon-Hull City Council, Sheffield City Council, South Lanarkshire District Council, Swansea City Council, Urban Splash, and Wigan Metropolitan Borough. Designers who provided information included Alsop Architects, Bauman Lyons, Camlin Lonsdale, CZWG Architects, Grafton Architects, Terry Farrell & Partners, Glenn Howells Architects, Paul Keogh Architects, McGarry Ni Eanaigh Architects, Page & Park, Nicholas Ray Associates and Urban Initiatives.

USING THE GUIDE

The places we describe are to be found throughout Britain and Ireland. To help those who are using the guide to plan visits, we have divided them into ten regional groups, shown on the map opposite. Each region has been given a number which corresponds to the section numbering used throughout the book. The regions are not equal in size and in some cases they do not follow established regional boundaries. Our main objective has been to provide the user with a group of places that can form a convenient cluster. Each of the regional groups is preceded by a short introduction. This describes the extent of the region, its major foci and any special characteristics. It also identifies places of note not included in the body of the guide, such as historic sites.

Individual places are described by a short text identifying the features that make it significant. The descriptive text also provides an opportunity to set out the reasons for the inclusion of the place and to identify links to nearby places. The location of the place is described and where possible the lead urban designer identified, together with the name of the relevant local authority.

The question of authorship of any urban-design scheme is often problematic. Good places are almost always the product of multi-disciplinary effort and are often created over a considerable period of time. As a reflection of this we have not identified individuals in the credits for each place but have noted the lead agency or consultaant. Almost by definition places include an element of the 'public realm' and as such local authorities are almost always closely involved in their creation and management. They are identified because of this pivotal role and for their potential as a source of further information.

1 **LONDON**

2 **SOUTH EAST**
East and West Sussex, Kent,
Surrey

3 **EAST**
Bedfordshire, Cambridgeshire,
Essex, Hertfordshire, Norfolk,
Suffolk

4 **SOUTH**
Berkshire, Buckinghamshire,
Hampshire, Isle of Wight,
Oxfordshire

5 **SOUTH WEST/SOUTH WALES**
Avon, Cornwall, Devon, Dorset,
Gloucestershire, Somerset,
Wiltshire, South Wales

6 **MIDLANDS**
Derbyshire, Herefordshire,
Leicestershire, Lincolnshire,
Nottinghamshire,
Northamptonshire,Shropshire,
Staffordshire, Warwickshire,
Worcestershire, West Midlands

7 **NORTH WEST/NORTH WALES**
Cheshire, Cumbria, Lancashire,
Greater Manchester,
Merseyside, North Wales

8 **NORTH**
Humberside, North Yorkshire,
South Yorkshire, West
Yorkshire, Cleveland, Durham,
Northumberland, Tyne and Wear

9 **SCOTLAND**

10 **IRELAND**

INTRODUCTION 1.2

BROADGATE 1.4

COVENT GARDEN 1.6

CAMDEN LOCK 1.8

CHINATOWN: GERRARD STREET 1.10

COMYN CHING TRIANGLE 1.12

DOCKLANDS: CANARY WHARF 1.14

DOCKLANDS: CROSSHARBOUR 1.16

DOCKLANDS: GREENLAND DOCK 1.18

EALING BROADWAY CENTRE 1.20

GABRIEL'S WHARF 1.22

HAY'S GALLERIA 1.24

KING'S ROAD: BLUEBIRD 1.26

LONDON

LEICESTER SQUARE 1.28

LILLINGTON STREET 1.30

NATIONAL THEATRE: THEATRE SQUARE 1.32

PECKHAM: TOWN SQUARE 1.34

PENGE HIGH STREET 1.36

RICHMOND RIVERSIDE 1.38

ST CHRISTOPHER'S PLACE 1.40

ST KATHERINE'S DOCK 1.42

SOMERSET HOUSE 1.44

TOWER BRIDGE PIAZZA 1.46

WANDSWORTH: BATTERSEA SQUARE 1.48

WESTBOURNE GROVE 1.50

WESTMINSTER CATHEDRAL PIAZZA 1.52

INTRODUCTION

The London region hardly needs definition but a boundary is necessary to assist in delimiting adjoining regions. We have followed the convention of defining it as being that area contained by the M25 motorway. Although geographically the region is the smallest in this guide, its population exceeds that of any other.

There are many historic places in London and new places are continually emerging. Most of the tourist hot-spots are sadly disappointing. Piccadilly Circus is no more than a traffic route. There are more positive signs that Trafalgar Square will become pedestrianised and develop towards being a 'World Square'. Improvement has already taken place in Leicester Square (page 1.28). There are places worth seeking out – the secret medieval city of the Temple south of the Strand and east of Somerset House (page 1.44), the gas-lit Dickensian street of Woburn Walk near Euston Station, Lincoln's Inn Fields and New Square – like the Temple the haunts of lawyers and retaining the quiet collegiate air of affluent 18th-century London.

London's railway stations have been undergoing a revival. The first was Liverpool Street, where the site of the rush for the train has been transformed to a brightly lit meeting place with links east across Bishopsgate to Spitalfields and west to Broadgate (page 1.4). Londoners are still waiting for the full redevelopment of Paddington and its adjoining basin. An exciting recent addition to transportation is the Jubilee Line extension, co-ordinated by Roland Paoletti, with stations at Westminster by Michael Hopkins, Bermondsey by MacCormac Jamieson Prichard, Canada Water by Eva Jiricna and Canary Wharf by Norman Foster almost good places themselves. A trip south leads to Cutty Sark Gardens and the World Heritage Site of Greenwich.

London's green spaces are a delight and a number of the royal parks are being remodelled. St James's Park is a good location from which to view the façades of the Mall,

Whitehall and the London Eye beyond. Regent's Park with its Nash terraces is a special pleasure. The set-pieces of London's parks are one aspect of green space but in Islington a railway line has been transformed into Gillespie Park while in Haringey a parkland walk has been created. Both bring greenery to deprived environments.

Down the Thames past the National Theatre (page 1.32), Tate Modern and the Globe Theatre have transformed the riverside and will, with Gabriel's Wharf (page 1.20), the refurbished Oxo Tower and the dampened Millennium Bridge, create significant additions to London's public spaces. Glass covering seems to have emerged as a genre. Hay's Galleria (page 1.24) is included here but Waterloo International station is not. Our justification is the single-use focus of Waterloo. A case could also be made for the inclusion of the British Museum's magnificent Great Court in Bloomsbury, one of London's significant quarters.

Outer London is often viewed as an urban desert. In fact, there are oases of urbanism. Southwark has invested heavily in the Peckham area (page 1.34) but most notable is Croydon, which rivals Canary Wharf in terms of its transatlantic character. The new tram system has heralded a change in the modelling of the town and Croydon is a place to watch. Further east, urban interventions are restoring the vitality of Penge (page 1.36). To the west there is the historic suburb of Bedford Park. Heathrow Airport dwarfs all around it, but to its north a reclaimed tip has provided a civilised working environment – Stockley Park. But for its virtually exclusive focus on work it would be a 'good place'.

Moving about London can be an adventure so we have provided an *AtoZ* reference, from edition 4 (1998, revised 2000). The referencing system can change between editions. We have noted underground stations and where possible buses.

BROADGATE

Few developments in Britain offer the quality of the public realm in the way that those in Paris or New York do. It is therefore particularly gratifying to find not one but two such places on a site with some of the highest land values in the country. Completed in the mid-1980s, it must be the City's only good development of that depressing decade. The fact that Stuart Lipton was the commissioning developer is reassuring vis-à-vis the Commission for Architecture and the Built Environment (CABE) where he was appointed as the first chairman.

The central circular space is surrounded by a series of office buildings with terraces and glass atria with abundant vegetation inside and out. Some of the ground floor is occupied by shops and restaurants. The central space is used as a skating rink in the winter and for various events for the rest of the year; it is particularly well used at lunchtime. The articulation between this space and the adjacent ones follows more closely the City's historic pattern than other post-war developments (such as the Barbican). A large Richard Serra sculpture marks the entrance from Liverpool Street station while to the north-west the link to Finsbury Square is at right angles, providing a surprise when walking from one into the other. Both spaces are pedestrianised. The materials used are of high quality and the public art is neither token nor condescending. Exchange Square, perhaps less successful, is on an adjacent site spanning the tracks running into Liverpool Street.

Nearby is the recently redeveloped Liverpool Street station; Spitalfields market is to the east, Richard Rogers' Lloyds Building in Leadenhall Street to the south, and John Soane's Bank of England to the west.

LOCATION Liverpool Street mainline and underground stations [*AtoZ* 6G 145]
LOCAL AUTHORITIES City of London and London Borough of Hackney

Arup Associates

COVENT GARDEN

People with an allergy to crowds should avoid this prime example of a vibrant dense urban environment. The history of the area started in the 17th century with the development of the square designed by Inigo Jones for the Duke of Bedford. A market immediately settled here and grew steadily. The subject of one of the great planning battles of the early 1970s when the fruit-and-vegetable market finally moved out of the area, it was saved from redevelopment and transformed into one of London's main attractions by the Greater London Council. Market buildings have been restored and converted for retail and entertainment: the present uses are perhaps not so different from those engraved by Hogarth. The central area and some of the surrounding streets have been pedestrianised and give the impression of a Mediterranean city, though critics may find similarities with a theme park. The recently reopened Royal Opera House, another planning battlefield, completes once again the original Inigo Jones square and while the quality of the scheme can be debated it does offer a new pedestrian link to the east and stunning views from its public terraces. Visitors should not miss the garden on the west side of St Paul's church, known as the actor's church, one of the few quiet oases in the area.

A bit further north and still in what is known as Covent Garden, Neal's Yard is another lively public space which acquired its character spontaneously, without a 'design'.

LOCATION Covent Garden is accessible by Underground, bus, on foot and bicycle: parking is virtually impossible [*AtoZ* 2F 149]
LOCAL AUTHORITY Westminster City Council

Greater London Council, Department of Architecture and Civic Design

CAMDEN LOCK

Camden Lock Market was opened in 1973 when what had been Dingwall's Timber Wharf and Dock was refurbished to provide space for new uses. The converted stables building, known as Dingwall's Gallery, formed the first part of the development. New buildings including a glazed atrium space have been added between this and Chalk Farm Road (a continuation of Camden High Street). A performance and seating area overlooks the canal and on adjacent sites many warehouses have been converted to residential use. At week-ends there is a very popular market with open-air stalls and in the evenings a stand-up comedy venue. The canalside walk connects through to Regent's Park and to the King's Cross area and a canal-boat service goes west to Little Venice. Further north along Chalk Farm Road is the Roundhouse, originally an engine shed for Euston station and now used as an arts venue.

On the southern side of the canal new development takes advantage of its location with a glazed frontage to Camden High Street. The development extends back to Jamestown Road where CZWG's Glasshouse building is a stunning combination of retail, restaurants and apartments.

LOCATION walk north up Camden High Street from Camden Town Underground station [*AtoZ* 7F 45]
LOCAL AUTHORITY London Borough of Camden

John Dickinson Architect

CHINATOWN: GERRARD STREET

Small businesses ply their trade, with restaurants not merely confined to ground floors but sometimes rising up four storeys. Elsewhere there are music shops, fishmongers, travel shops, booksellers, supermarkets, hairdressers, solicitors, Chinese herbal chemists, public houses, as well as residential accommodation on many upper floors. Three Chinese 'gateways' mark the entrances to Gerrard Street from the east, west and north. Through-traffic was excluded from the street and its repaving and furnishing created a pedestrian ambience. The rather kitsch street furniture exudes a Chinese signature. Street names are in both English and Chinese characters. Two Chinese dragon sculptures 'guard' the street commemorating the scheme. These symbolic cues add layers of visual and cultural interest contributing to the 'sense of place'.

However, it is the people and their activities that really characterise Chinatown. Nowhere else in London is there such a concentration of oriental peoples going about their everyday business, buying food from the local supermarkets, or simply eating *dim sum* or other delicacies. The area is now a popular tourist destination. At Chinese New Year (around January or February) and Moon Cake Festival (August) Chinatown is the focus of festivities and activities, and flags and banners are draped across the street and adorn buildings.

LOCATION Underground to Leicester Square, north up Charing Cross Road, left into Little Newport Street and on to Gerrard Street [*AtoZ* 2D 148]
LOCAL AUTHORITY Westminster City Council

Westminster City Council

COMYN CHING TRIANGLE

Protected from the bustle of Covent Garden (page 1.6), Comyn Ching is an idyllic spot nestling within the rich relics of three historic façades. The scheme is a public courtyard that gives a specific identity and focus of activity to an urban block.

The main feature of the redevelopment for Comyn Ching, the ironmongery company, was the carving out of a new public courtyard, Ching Court, from what was a fully developed triangular site. The rear elevations of the buildings had to be transformed into suitable backdrops for the new public space. Entrances were established to attract the public into and through an area that had previously been private – the courtyard provides a diagonal public route from Seven Dials to Shelton Street. Concern with detail was intensified by the scale and enclosed nature of the courtyard. A series of features was used to generate interest at ground level and to reduce the potentially oppressive effect of the narrow courtyard space: three office entrances with large projecting porches arranged against the rear of Monmouth Street, inspired by 18th-century design; a rear passage entrance from Shelton Street flanked by large rear windows of shop units; two trees; and a Lutyens' seat on Mercer Street. Existing terraces were restored and three new corner buildings constructed.

The scheme contains the traditional diversity of uses found in the city, with one side for residential use, one side for offices and the third with shops on the ground floor and residential use above. Close by are Covent Garden and Neal Street.

LOCATION Underground to Covent Garden north up Neal Street, left into Shelton Street; the Comyn Ching Triangle is to the right [*AtoZ* 1E 148]
LOCAL AUTHORITY Westminster City Council

Terry Farrell and Partners

DOCKLANDS: CANARY WHARF

In the centre of the central part of the Isle of Dogs in the middle of Docklands is Canary Wharf. Standing sentinel-like over the area is Cesar Pelli's Canary Wharf Tower. Emerging from the Jubilee Line via Foster's cavernous and Piranesian new station, the immediate impression is of the intimidating power of commerce. This appears to be a place dominated by the large scale. Canary Wharf Tower is the tallest building in Britain and around its feet are buildings whose major preoccupation seems to be security. But this is security in a smart suit. Everywhere there are high-quality materials and careful detailing. Underlying the thrusting architecture is a masterplan by SOM. Cabot Place East is linked via the glass-vaulted Docklands Light Railway (DLR) station to an underground shopping centre, Cabot Square West. Up into the air and the fountains of Cabot Square play. There are a few highly controlled trees regimented to march down West India Avenue and to the comparative greenery of West Ferry Circus.

On a wet day it can all be rather bleak. Can this really be a good place? Then the sun comes out, light plays on the water, there are tables outside, people relaxing in the wine bars and cafés that cluster like blossom at the foot of the blocks. Perhaps it is a good place after all. Then there are the bridges: the floating bridge across West India Dock, the curving bridge across Limekiln Dock to the Limehouse residential area. A Docklands Light Railway train clatters like a fairground ride to Heron Quay. Somehow the image of *Metropolis* returns. This is a place you love or hate. Whichever, it is a place well worth a visit.

LOCATION Underground or DLR to Canary Wharf – go by one, return by the other perhaps [*AtoZ* 1C 80]
LOCAL AUTHORITY London Borough of Tower Hamlets

masterplan Skidmore Owings and Merrill (SOM)

DOCKLANDS: CROSSHARBOUR

Descend from Crossharbour station, in the heart of the Isle of Dogs, turn west into Pepper Street and providing there is not an event on at the adjoining London Arena you have entered a haven of quiet. The almost fairground-like cacophony of the former enterprise zone recedes. There is a colonnaded walk, small shops, several bars, offices and tantalising views of the old Millwall Inner Dock. This is an intimate environment where, in spite of the occasional delivery van, pedestrians and cyclists rule. Glengall Bridge links either side of Millwall Dock and Pepper Street re-establishes a strategic cross-island route both for pedestrians and, almost uniquely in Docklands, for cyclists. Small plane trees soften the scene and a spritsail barge or two delight the nautical eye. Only when the eye turns north and heavenwards does the bulk of Canary Wharf (page 1.8) stand out as a reminder of the commercial world nearby.

LOCATION Crossharbour station on the Docklands Light Railway [*AtoZ* 3D 80]
LOCAL AUTHORITY London Borough of Tower Hamlets

London Docklands Development Corporation

DOCKLANDS: GREENLAND DOCK

Established in 1699 as the Howland Great Wet Dock, Greenland Dock was one of the first parts of the London Docklands Development area to be brought forward for redevelopment. The objective in 1981 was to transform 36 hectares of apparently hopeless dereliction in an unfashionable part of London. After having dealt with methane contamination and repaired the dock structures, the area now has fine waterside vistas and views to Canary Wharf to the east and Greenwich to the south. As well as 1200 houses, it contains a watersports centre, shops, a pub and a new marina. The housing includes groups of distinctive character, each defining new streets and public areas. Water plays a significant part in the character of the site from the bustle of the marina to the quiet waterside walks. In the Finland Quay area, Norway Dock has been developed as an ecological park.

With 27 development sites. a strong urban design framework was needed and this was provided by a clear masterplan and the consistent use of paving and landscaping; special concrete-block paving was developed for the site and this has been employed with granite setts and York stone paving. It is encouraging that almost half of the housing is occupied by people originally from the area. Nearby is Canada Water station on the Jubilee Line (opened in 1999); Greenwich is about 3 kilometres east.

LOCATION Surrey Quays Underground, then Redriff Road (A2202) around the north or Plough Way around the south of the area [*AtoZ* 3A 80]
LOCAL AUTHORITY London Borough of Southwark

masterplan Conran Roche

EALING BROADWAY CENTRE

The Centre was completed in 1984 and comprises two enclosed shopping malls leading from existing streets to a large open courtyard called Town Square.

An earlier proposal in the late 1970s was rejected following opposition by numerous local groups under the 'Ealing Alliance' umbrella. Their objection related to the scale, design and consequent destruction of Ealing's close-knit 19th-century townscape. The local council then prepared a planning brief in consultation with the Ealing Civic Society and other local associations. The brief set out the principle to be followed, which included a more modest development, provision of an open square, no relief road and the use of brick and slate in order to blend with the surrounding style. The outcome is a deliberately picturesque design. The Town Square and street frontages are faced with brick and the scheme includes decorative ironwork to the openings in the multi-storey carpark and to the staircase which rises between twin towers. The Town Square provides access to the main public library reached by staircase to the upper level. There is thus a very simple combination of commercial and public space that attracts huge numbers every day, and especially at weekends, and that people clearly feel comfortable in. Whenever the weather is reasonable the central square is thronged with people standing, sitting or talking. Sometimes the space gets let to small stall traders selling craft items; sometimes there is entertainment. The Town Square has recently been redesigned but retains its essential character.

LOCATION Ealing Broadway Underground and mainline station [*AtoZ* 7D 56]
LOCAL AUTHORITY Ealing Borough Council

Building Design Partnership (BDP)

GABRIEL'S WHARF

Coin Street Community Builders was formed in 1984 as a not-for-profit public service. Its aim was to seek improvements to the South Bank that would benefit the community rather than the alternative private development scheme of offices, shopping and apartments that was being proposed. It bought 5.25 hectares of land occupied by derelict buildings and now manages Gabriel's Wharf, Oxo Tower Wharf, Bernie Spain Gardens and a section of the riverside walk.

Although only seen as a temporary development, Gabriel's Wharf has become a highly popular venue for local workers, residents and visitors. The blank wall of the London Studios, which forms the western edge to the site, was painted like a screen set to provide an interesting backdrop. The design of the individual units is unadventurous but the mixture of uses – crafts, bars and restaurants with a lot of outdoor dining – is compelling – when the weather is good. Adjacent to this, the nine-storey Oxo Tower Wharf was completely refurbished to provide shops and craft outlets at ground and first floor with a rooftop restaurant and brasserie. Further west along the riverside walk is the National Theatre (page 1.32) where a new entrance space has been created as part of work to improve front-of-house facilities.

LOCATION to the east of the National Theatre, accessible from the riverside walk. Waterloo or Southwark Underground [*AtoZ* 4J 149]
LOCAL AUTHORITY Lambeth Borough Council

John Dickinson Architect

HAY'S GALLERIA

1.24

It is more than ten years since Hay's Galleria opened. Created by the simple yet inspired device of erecting a soaring barrel roof spanning between the curving 19th-century buildings on either side, it has made a year-round ordered space, comparable, though without the baroque carved-stone embellishment, to that of its Italian namesake. Combining historic architecture on an heroic scale with innovation in its adaptation, the high quality of both the new work and the restorations together with an engaging range of uses makes for an experience which can delight worker, cultural tourist and foodie. You can browse the attractive shops and market stalls, enjoy lunch, and admire the panoramic river views. At the central plaza stands David Kemp's *The Navigator*, a magnificent 18-metre-high kinetic sculpture, a hypnotic combination of moving parts, water jets and grand fountains.

Hay's Wharf is part of the London Bridge City commercial riverside development and provides office space, a landscaped riverside walk, tourist information office and pier, all of which give it a steady and sizeable visitor base. Nearby are the Tower of London, Tower Bridge, HMS 'Belfast', the Design Museum, Southwark Cathedral and Tate Modern at Bankside. The Galleria is only open Monday to Friday, 9.00–18.30, Saturday, 9.00–17.00, and Sunday, 11.00–17.00.

LOCATION Underground or rail to London Bridge. From Westminster Pier by boat, taking in many other riverside attractions on the way [*AtoZ* 4G 151]
LOCAL AUTHORITY London Borough of Southwark

Twigg Brown and Partners

KING'S ROAD: BLUEBIRD

Built in 1923, the Bluebird garage was then Europe's largest facility. The fabric and structure of the building have been sensitively restored with contemporary elements inserted with care. The forecourt has been repaved in setts and stone and a sleek steel and glass fruit-and- vegetable stall gives a flamboyant focus to the attractive courtyard. The multiplicity of activities and the positive use of the forecourt adds liveliness to one of London's interesting streets where design shops, antiques and fashion outlets rub shoulders with fashionable cafés and restaurants. A clear example where the design quality of the glazed canopy adds value to the space it occupies. As a result Bluebird has enlivened and enhanced the amenities of King's Road.

Battersea Square (page 1.48) can be visited by walking across Battersea Bridge and along by the new Montevetro apartments (Richard Rogers Partnership).

LOCATION on the north side of King's Road, west of Beaufort Street. Sloane Square Underground and then bus, or long walk from South Kensington Underground station [*AtoZ* 6B 76]
LOCAL AUTHORITY Royal Borough of Kensington and Chelsea

CD Partnership

LEICESTER SQUARE

Leicester Square, regenerated through its closure to traffic, is again a good place to see and to be seen in. Outdoor tables and chairs in traffic-free streets, a central green oasis, street entertainment, continuous active frontages of clubs, restaurants, hotels and bars around London's thriving cinema centre. A destination, a place to linger, sit or pass through. These positive features were absent prior to a comprehensive design initiative.

In 1989, after nearly 300 years as a traffic roundabout, this historic garden square became London's largest pedestrian zone. Today the area has all the characteristics of urban vitality and economic viability so sought after by politicians and planners. By contrast, in the 1980s the square was a shabby focus for the worst excesses of the Soho vice industry with the central gardens a gloomy, virtual no-go area of mugging, drug-taking and prostitution. The modest landscape solutions included restoring diagonal routes, upgrading lighting for safe 24-hour activity and providing uncluttered durable surfaces to cope with large volumes of pedestrians. The main innovations included the first Westminster CCTV public-realm monitoring system and on-site management accommodation. All this was achieved without the traffic controversy experienced by other proposals. Existing legislation for traffic management was used for a comprehensive scheme of restrictions to the square and all approach streets.

Ironically, today's economic success has raised new local concerns over the negative effects of over-intensive use, perhaps forgetting the very serious original problems overcome by an urban design approach to creating a good place.

LOCATION east of Piccadilly Circus, west of Charing Cross Road, north of the National Gallery [*AtoZ* 3D 148]
LOCAL AUTHORITY Westminster City Council

Westminster City Council

LILLINGTON STREET

One of the largest comprehensive redevelopments in post-war London, Lillington Street provides 945 dwellings for more than 2000 residents. Although predominantly housing, Lillington Street (also known as Longmore Gardens Village), contains delightful tree-filled public spaces, a parade of shops, three pubs, a medical centre, branch library, tennis courts, playgrounds, community facilities and an old people's home. Access to the 'village' is provided by five bus stops on its periphery and the nearby Pimlico Underground station. Integrated into the scheme is the Victorian church of St James-the-less. The church's red brick provides the cue to the aesthetic that guides the whole 4.5-hecatre estate. The scheme derived from a 1961 competition won by John Darbourne. There were three award-winning phases linked by an overall impression of small scale and the use of a restrained palette of materials. The housing blocks define the external streetscape and the internal green courtyards. The blocks have a varied roofline and planting is provided on high-level walkways, softening the appearance of the internal areas. The area was designated a Conservation Area in 1990 and the majority of the buildings are listed as Grade II*. This may control individual expression now that 30 per cent of the estate is owner-occupied.

Nearby is Churchill Square Housing (Powell and Moya, 1949); Tate Britain is less than a kilometre to the south-east.

LOCATION Underground to Pimlico; several bus services, including No. 24 running down adjoining Vauxhall Bridge Road [*AtoZ* 4B 154]
LOCAL AUTHORITY Westminster City Council

Darbourne and Darke

NATIONAL THEATRE: THEATRE SQUARE

When Denys Lasdun's brutalist theatre opened in 1975 it was described by its deputy director as being a '...mixture of Gatwick Airport and Brent Cross Shopping Centre...'. With the furore surrounding the architectural style of the building itself, little attention was paid to the area around it. A start on improving this situation was made with the designation of the Queen's Walk from Waterloo to Tower Bridge. Moving from the fortress of the South Bank Centre (will this area finally be saved by Rick Mather's proposals?), through the gateway arches of Waterloo Bridge, one enters a world of second-hand-book stalls and river views. Then there are trees and seats and the bulk of the theatre rises to the south. What was previously part of a service road dividing the theatre from the riverside has been closed; the area provides extended box-office facilities and a bookshop, and externally a new public space emphasised by lighting, seating and people-friendly materials. In front there are changes in level and in summer an audience of seats shaped like people waits in anticipation for the next performance. This is Theatre Square. At times a quiet refuge from the bustle of the riverside, at others a riot of activity, on summer evenings the gathering place of the chardonnay-sipping glitterati waiting for another first night, it can still be a gloomy place – a problem of all spaces where main views are to the north. But what views across the river: the cliff-like frontage of Somerset House (page 1.44) sparkles in the sun and further east the towers and minarets of the Temple rise like a secret city.

Theatre Square demonstrates how simple level changes, honest planting and good materials can transform a space into a place.

LOCATION Underground to Waterloo East then follow the signs to South Bank. Mainline to Waterloo and Waterloo International [*AtoZ* 4H 149]
LOCAL AUTHORITY London Borough of Lambeth

Stanton Williams Associates

PECKHAM: TOWN SQUARE

An arched fabric cover on Peckham High Street provides one of the entrances to an imaginative group of public buildings and associated uses. Peckham Library by Alsop and Störmer, which won the RIBA Stirling Prize in 2000, provides a covered area which is oversailed by the fourth-floor level where most of the library space is located. Pods of special activity areas project above roof level – an audacious vermilion 'beret' which, together with the external copper cladding, indicates that the architects believe that the public domain is enriched by strong forms and vivid colours.

Peckham Pulse, a healthy-living centre, is located on an adjacent site and this provides leisure, nutrition, health and education facilities under one roof. A Wetherspoon's family pub also forms part of the development. The hard landscape, somewhat undefined as a space, connects these buildings together with black, grey and buff stone with strings of material crossing the area and accentuated by lighting. The area below the arched fabric cover is often used for an informal market at the weekends.

The development of the whole area has been seen by the London Borough of Southwark as a means of contributing to the economic regeneration of the area.

LONDON

LOCATION close to the junction of Peckham High Street and Peckham Hill Street [*AtoZ* 1G 95]
LOCAL AUTHORITY London Borough of Southwark

landscape design Southwark Building Design Services

PENGE: HIGH STREET

Three small new town 'squares' using 'time' as the design theme, have been introduced into Penge High Street. They were created between 1999 and 2001 as part of the revitalisation of the town centre and as part of the Crystal Palace Partnership Programme. The main 'square', called the Penge Triangle, terminates the High Street and is bounded by the post office, cafés, shops and the Crooked Billet pub. The space centres on a steel and glass clock-shelter which forms a focal structure in the street. Its canopy was inspired by the wings of the pterodactyl, one of the Victorian monsters in nearby Crystal Palace Park. Through traffic, except for buses, was removed and the footway widened to create an outdoor sitting area for café trade. A line of globe-headed trees defines the space and creates pedestrian scale, and the area is enhanced at night by dramatic lighting.

Arpley Square, 50 metres along the High Street, was enclosed using an ornamental 5-metre-high metal screen designed by Geraldine Konyn, with ideas from local children. The square centres on a pavement maze and performance space. Sculptures by Mark Folds, depicting a dinosaur landscape, form very popular seating for children.

Empire Square, 70 metres further south along the High Street, has a series of dramatic tensile structures by architects Stock Woolstencroft. These link the shopping arcade to the High Street, providing shelter for sitting and community events. Colourful murals, designed by Annabelle Dawson with ideas from local school children, depict Penge past, present and future. They enliven the square together with feature lighting, striking paving patterns and new retail signage.

LOCATION at the junction of the A234 and Maple Road; mainline station Penge East [*AtoZ* 7J 111]

LOCAL AUTHORITY London Borough of Bromley

Philip Cave Associates

RICHMOND RIVERSIDE

This redevelopment occupies a major site in a historic town next to the Thames. Success must therefore be measured in terms of the fact that such an opportunity was not lost but taken as the cue for a relevant and striking exercise in urban design. Respectful of the street pattern, the layout presents an appropriate scale along Hill Street and facing the Thames and on the links between them. A particular feature is the way a series of individual buildings are expressed by changes in design and facing materials. This and respect for the urban grain ensures that the surviving buildings from the past blend with their new surroundings. In turn, the development relates well to the town centre, reinforcing its character.

Another feature is the mixed range of uses, including shops, offices, residential, public houses and a small cinema. There is also a large landscaped area overlooking the river. The detailed design is based, not without criticism, on a variety of neoclassical themes, generally handled in a sensitive and articulate way and responding to the context. The requirements of servicing and parking do not detract from the overall quality. It connects well into Richmond's structure and it can be approached from a number of directions including the route from Richmond station via George Street and the riverside which forms part of the Thames Path.

Kew Botanical Gardens are about 1.6 kilometres north, as are Syon Park and Richmond Park.

LOCATION Richmond Underground and mainline stations [AtoZ 5D 88]
LOCAL AUTHORITY London Borough of Richmond

Quinlan Terry Associates

ST CHRISTOPHER'S PLACE

St Christopher's Place lies between Wigmore Street to Oxford Street and was developed in the mid to late 19th century. Gee's Court, the entrance from Oxford Street, is so narrow that its discovery is a surprise. On entry sheer delight unveils itself. The four-storey mixed-use buildings create a strong sense of enclosure The space emerges into Barrett Street with its shops, restaurants and apartments. Piers define the entrance to the place from James Street and a William Pye sculpture and water feature forms the focus of the street which was landscaped in 1993. The footway has been extended for alfresco eating; even in winter, tables and chairs outside are occupied. North of this space, Victorian terraces flank St Christopher's Place. The view northwards is framed by a taller building in Wigmore Street. Back from this the entrance to St Christopher's Place is defined by an arch. The street is paved with York stone. At Christmas time the area is festooned with lights and decorations. A jazz festival runs from July to September.

Nearby are The Wallace Collection in Manchester Square and Saarinen's US Embassy in Grosvenor Square.

LOCATION between Oxford Street and Wigmore Street. Bond Street Underground station is on the opposite side of Oxford Street [*AtoZ* 7H 141]
LOCAL AUTHORITY Westminster City Council

Townshend Landscape Architects

ST KATHERINE'S DOCK

This proves the point that a place can be good even though the large majority of buildings that enclose it are mediocre. Only two, Ivy House (Thomas Aitcheson, 1854), converted to mixed uses and the Dockmaster's house (1828) at the side of the lock remain from the original enclosed dock developed between 1824 and 1828, when some 1200 homes were demolished and 11,000 people made homeless. Never very successful, the docks closed in 1966 and the area converted to provide a yacht marina, a business and tourist centre and some housing. The original scheme, which preceded the creation of the London Docklands Development Corporation by more than ten years, was prepared under the aegis of the Greater London Council and included some social housing. The paving and street furniture retain the original marine and industrial character of the dock and some public art attempts to emphasise the same theme. The much-photographed Dickens Inn is a new construction using part of the timber structure of an adjacent warehouse which was demolished. Other buildings vary from brutalist to postmodern. In spite of the architectural jumble, the area is lively, arguably because its main attraction, the water, is also the most genuine. People like wandering at the water's edge, observing the craft going through the lock or getting refreshments in the theme park atmosphere of the Inn and other establishments which overlook the marina. The mix seems to work better than in most London Docklands public spaces.

LOCATION Underground to Tower Hill. St Katherine's Dock is signposted [*AtoZ* 4K 151]
LOCAL AUTHORITY London Borough of Tower Hamlets

Andrew Renton and Associates

SOMERSET HOUSE

Well-defined gateways are a key characteristic of a good place. Somerset House has four gateways and has such well-defined boundaries that it forms an enclosed world of its own. Why should we include what appears to be a single building as a good place? Somerset House was originally built as offices for various government departments including the Navy. In its original form these offices, designed by Sir William Chambers, focused on a central square flanked by two 'streets' on the east and west . Its architectural style was relentlessly classical and the full language of classicism – archways, flights of stairs and strategically placed sculptures – was used. In many ways it was the Broadgate of its day (1796). Two hundred years of government use did not serve the complex well and in the 1990s the great central court was nothing more than a carpark. An awareness campaign and the advent of resources from the Heritage Lottery Fund combined with some rationalisation of the Inland Revenue allowed the cars to be cleared and new uses, including the Courtauld Gallery and the Gilbert Collection of furniture and silver, to be installed. A definable and individual space became a vibrant public place. This was further enhanced by the introduction of cafés and open-air eating places both in the central area and on the terrace overlooking the Thames. The final crowning glory was the installation of a grid of capricious fountains playfully rising and falling in the summer. For a short period during the winter the fountains are replaced with a skating rink. This is a truly splendid transformation, a haven of humanity away from the roar of traffic in the Strand and the Embankment.

LOCATION Underground to Embankment. Access from the south is via Waterloo Bridge and the Embankment. From the north access is from the Strand [*AtoZ* 3G 149]
LOCAL AUTHORITY Westminster City Council

Donald Insall Associates/Dixon Jones/Inskip & Jenkins

TOWER BRIDGE PIAZZA

The scheme, sometimes known as Horselydown Square, is entered from the junction of Horselydown Lane and Shad Thames, a short distance from the southern end of Tower Bridge. The three new buildings around the square accommodate shopping, a gallery and cafés at ground floor and the two five-storey buildings provide four storeys of flats above this. A building of seven storeys includes a first floor of commercial and office uses with flats above this. A fourth side to the square consists of the refurbishment of an existing structure to provide mainly residential accommodation. The angled entry to the square from Shad Thames with its rounded features and red render encourages people to move into the space. The main material is brick and the floorscape is simply designed with a central water feature, complete with nymphs, and seating that complements the building design.

Adjacent is Shad Thames which retains its Victorian character of a narrow street with walkways above that were used to connect the original warehouses. Today the buildings serve a new range of uses with restaurants, galleries and shops mainly at ground level and housing above. The Design Museum, well worth a visit, is located further down Shad Thames and the riverside walk continues beyond this point connected across an inlet dock to New Concordia Wharf and points east, an attractive detour.

LOCATION junction of Horselydown Lane and Shad Thames. London Bridge or Tower Hill Underground [*AtoZ* 6J 151]
LOCAL AUTHORITY London Borough of Southwark

Julyan Wickham and Associates

WANDSWORTH: BATTERSEA SQUARE

This site has been known as Battersea Square since the 18th century; it housed the village pump. Derelict since the 1970s, reconstruction of its surviving early- and mid-19th-century buildings was conceived and guided by a conservation brief prepared for Wandsworth Council. Residents and businesses were consulted on proposals which included permissions for restaurants and cafés to spill on to the square, a new fountain, stone paving, new lighting and well-positioned trees that form a canopy over the square in summer, all won back from wall-to-wall roadway. This is one of the rare situations where a local authority has successfully sponsored an emergent public realm. This project has made a piazza that is truly enjoyable to be in and prompted the regeneration of the surrounding area.

LOCATION Clapham Junction mainline station is to the south. Take Falcon Road and Battersea High Street to the Square [*AtoZ* 1B 92]
LOCAL AUTHORITY London Borough of Wandsworth

Wandsworth Borough Council

WESTBOURNE GROVE

1.50

Notting Hill's funkiest public lavatory, this imaginative design combines utility with a sense of place. A triangular space provided the opportunity to redevelop the existing public lavatories and integrate them into a flower shop ingeniously designed to provide a focal point within the space. It might, however, have been very different as the local authority filled in the previous underground lavatory and eventually published proposals for its replacement. The local community took exception to the proposals and commissioned CZWG to provide an alternative within the council's budget. The idea of including a flower kiosk was added to the brief by the residents, as was the clock which was donated by the community.

The site is known as 'Turquoise Island' as tiles of that colour envelop the triangular base for the building and provide a platform for displaying flowers. The Parisian-type glazed canopy and the public clock combine with the glazed tiles to provide a brilliant response to an unusual site. Tree planting and oversized public seats complement this idiosyncratic response to an individual situation. The terraces on either side include interesting galleries and antique shops.

The wider area includes the fascinating Portobello Street market and streets of spacious Victorian dwellings.

LONDON

LOCATION Westbourne Grove and Colville Road junction [*AtoZ* 6H 59]
LOCAL AUTHORITY Royal Borough of Kensington and Chelsea

CZWG Architects

WESTMINSTER CATHEDRAL PIAZZA

When redevelopment of the Victoria Street frontage occurred in the late 1970s the opportunity was taken to open up a view of the north front of the Catholic cathedral with its exuberant and exotically striped façade and campanile. The cathedral, completed in 1903, was designed by J F Bentley in the Byzantine style at the request of Cardinal Vaughan, possibly to avoid competition with Westminster Abbey. The interior includes stations of the cross by Eric Gill. The flanking development with its bold crystalline shapes steps down towards the piazza but the microclimate is still affected adversely. There are views from the cathedral's campanile (open 9.30–17.00). The piazza, which is located over an underground carpark, was repaved in 1994 using York stone laid to a parabolic curve. The layout provides a simple stone-paved area with well-designed bollards and lighting but it could be vastly improved if appropriate uses could be found for the outdoor space at ground level. The exotic north façade is seen to particular effect when it is floodlit and the piazza takes on an oriental quality in distinct contrast to the character of noisy Victoria Street.

LOCATION south side of Victoria Street next to Ambrosden Avenue. Victoria Underground station [*AtoZ* 2A 154]
LOCAL AUTHORITY Westminster City Council

Hyder Consulting Ltd

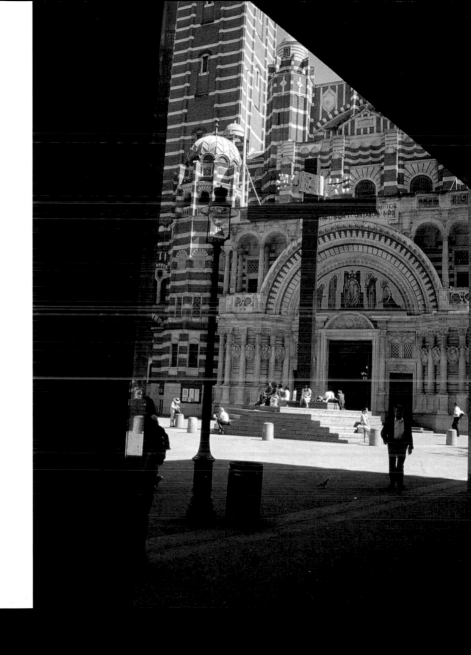

SOUTH-EAST ENGLAND

INTRODUCTION 2.2
BRIGHTON BEACH 2.4
BRIGHTON: THE LANES 2.6
CHICHESTER: PEDESTRIAN AREA 2.8
FARNHAM: LION AND LAMB YARD 2.10
HASTINGS: TOWN CENTRE 2.12
HORSHAM: CARFAX AND WEST STREET 2.14
NEW ASH GREEN: VILLAGE CENTRE 2.16
WHITSTABLE: FISHERMEN'S BUILDINGS 2.18

INTRODUCTION

This section covers the counties of Kent, East and West Sussex and Surrey. The region is strongly influenced by the proximity of London and transport routes reflect a focus on the capital. There are no good road links tying the region together and all too often it is necessary to travel inland to the M25 to get from one part of it to another. By rail the magnetic pull of London is even stronger.

The form of the region can be likened to sections of a clock face whose centre is London. Kent starts with the Thames Estuary at three o'clock and runs to half past four. East Sussex runs until six at which point West Sussex takes over and runs to seven. Surrey interposes itself between West Sussex and London. Each slice has its own character but all except Surrey are marked by their coastal nature. There are good places at Whitstable (page 2.18), Hastings (page 2.12) and Brighton (pages 2.4 and 2.6). The presence of the sea and its capacity for links to continental Europe gave rise to some of the most attractive historic places in the region. Sandwich in Kent – in Tudor times one of England's most important ports – survives now as an Elizabethan gem complete with a tiny central square known as the Cattle Market. Nearby is the Roman Richborough Castle with the remains of remarkable flint walls up to 4 metres thick and 8 metres high. It was from Richborough that Watling Street, the main Roman road, led via Rochester on the Medway to London and on to Chester. Further to the west along the coast is Rye, another one-time port but now only a calling place for yachts and fishermen. The small town with its steep cobbled streets now lies 1.6 kilometres inland. Within the town walls are a wealth of historic buildings. About the same distance inland is the medieval new town of Winchelsea, built on a grid plan.

The proximity of the sea and its healthy connotations prompted the 18th-century phenomenon of the resort town. Brighton claims to be the first: the exotic Brighton Pavilion and the Regency terraces of Kemptown and Hove mark its popularity with Regency England. Quieter and more genteel are Eastbourne to the east and Worthing to the west. Inland is the resort of Tunbridge Wells with its Pantiles, an 18th-century pedestrian mall, popularised by Beau Nash in the Regency period.

If the region has a unifying physical characteristic, it is the line of chalk hills that make up the North and South Downs. These formed an ancient highway linking Winchester (page 4.18) with Canterbury. Chichester (page 2.8) sits between the downs and the sea. Horsham (page 2.14), Guildford and Farnham (page 2.10) represent the wealth of the old market towns sited on the region's sandstone spine.

New Ash Green (page 2.16) and Crawley are products of the 20th-century planning system and owe their existence almost entirely to the need to house people from London. Crawley was the second government-sponsored new town to be established in the post-war period. New Ash Green was privately promoted but, like Crawley, follows closely the locational proposals for new satellite towns made by Patrick Abercrombie in his 1944 Greater London Plan. Almost 10 per cent of the UK's population lives and works in this region. It is subject to severe pressures for development and only by the very strict application of green-belt and strategic-gap principles is the distinctive character of its settlements maintained.

BRIGHTON BEACH

Brighton has a reputation for glamour tinged with scandal. The elegance of the Regency terraces is countered by the whiff of naughty weekends. England's seaside resorts have suffered decline. The area between Brighton's piers was particularly affected, compounded by the demise of the local fishing fleet, and the perceived unsuitability of the brick arches forming a backdrop to the beach. In 1992 a study from KPMG identified a seafront development strategy. The proposals were embraced by the council and a multidisciplinary approach adopted. The long-term objective was to use the redevelopment of the front as a stimulus for a general improvement in the city's fortunes and self-interest through better use of the arches it owned. A plan for the whole front was drawn up by Fiona Atkinson, then with the borough council. This broke the length into phases that could both relate to the availability of funding and to a chain of interrelated themes. These start from an historic theme focused on the old fish market and the fishing museum now housed in the arches. Moving west, smaller, less commercially viable arches are let on special terms to artists providing they both worked and sold from them. Further west a more active and noisy area reflects the nightclubs of the hinterland. Closer to Hove activity becomes more family biased. Particularly popular is the beach volley-ball court, essential on a pebbly beach. These uses are linked by strong curvilinear forms of paving and boarding complemented by special street furniture and by sculptures signposting key locations.

The multidisciplinary approach has resulted in every pound of public investment stimulating six from private funds – a fine example of public and private profit and pleasure through design.

LOCATION from Brighton station straight down Queens Road and West Street
LOCAL AUTHORITY Brighton and Hove City Council

Brighton Borough Council

BRIGHTON: THE LANES

The basic pattern of The Lanes is of a narrow grid into which have been inserted developments of shops and flats. Recently a pseudo-baroque office development and bland but monstrous council offices and hotel have rather marred the scene. The Lanes have a clear identity with a difference between the pattern of spaces in the original grid and later streets and squares, and the older cottage scale of buildings. The 19th-century buildings here – town hall, chapels, pubs, and some elegant town houses – provide the accent. Of the modern developments, Brighton Square is a textbook example of 1960s' townscape, its larger windows and regular plan hardly noticeable (the new fountain is too big and too exactly centred); Dukes Lane is more recent repro-chic. The 1980s' Regency Arcade has lost its faded air in a glossy refit and gained a new connection into The Lanes. The two modern monsters are easy to spot. Bartholomew Square is cold, shadowed and nearly always empty, while Nile Street's concrete baroque seems hard to let.

The identity of The Lanes comes as much from the uses and the street activity as from the spaces themselves. The narrow passages, the scale and complexity of the spaces serve to emphasise the shop displays. There is pavement dining and street musicians creating an exemplary serial vision. There is little sense of urgency; most people here have time and money to spend. Pubs, restaurants and clubs extend these patterns into the night. Brighton Pavilion, Regency Hove (west) and Kemptown (east) are all worth a detour.

LOCATION from Brighton station, down Queens Road towards the sea, past the clock tower, left from West Street into Dukes Street and The Lanes are ahead
LOCAL AUTHORITY Brighton and Hove City Council

Fitzroy Robinson and Partners (Brighton Square)

CHICHESTER: PEDESTRIAN AREA

Past decline left Chichester with a heritage of quiet domestic architecture. Roman origins bequeathed a simple crossroads plan. But a market cross at the crossing point presented a car-borne problem. Pedestrianisation was a solution and Chichester has escaped the superfluity of signs that have spoiled many good schemes. The buildings that frame the streets are a muddle of ages and styles. Most are despoiled by standardised corporate shopfronts. Near the Cross are two late-20th-century examples. At the corner of North Street and East Street is one, spoiled by a 'new' shopfront. Opposite, where South Street and West Street meet, is a more strident example.

West Street, with its cobbled carriageway and York stone footways, is an area where some vehicles are permitted. Facing the cathedral are converted buildings, the former Dolphin and Anchor Hotel, now shops, pub and a controversial fast-food outlet. A department store occupies a former school and a chapel now echoes to beer-drinking in a contentious pub. In East Street the surface is mainly York stone. There are ample cycle racks but pedestrians rule during the day. In the evening cyclists may use this area – time zoning encourages 'out-of-hours' use. Cobbles and a pinch point mark the car's return. Entertainers perform in the four main streets and cafés use the paving. What was a congested traffic route is a lively place in which to stroll.

Chichester Festival Theatre, 'The Pallants' (including Pallant House Gallery), Singleton Open Air Museum, 10 kilometres north on the A286, and Fishbourne Roman Palace, 1.5 kilometres west on the A259, are within easy reach.

LOCATION from Chichester station turn north up South Street. There are ample peripheral carparks off the A27

LOCAL AUTHORITY Chichester District Council

West Sussex County Council

FARNHAM: LION AND LAMB YARD

To insert a new shopping complex into a conservation area is one of the urban designer's most challenging tasks. Farnham is one of Surrey's most historic and admired towns and its Lion and Lamb Yard has Tudor origins. Yet it was into this setting in the 1980s that Lyons+Sleeman+Hoare were asked to insert 26 shops, a supermarket and office space. Partly a refurbishment and renovation exercise, partly new buildings, the completed Lion and Lamb Yard serves to link West Street, one of the main commercial streets in Farnham, to both short- and long-term carparks built on redundant backland. Completed in 1986, the courtyard and its public through route perpetuated the essentially medieval street pattern of the town, which has remained almost unchanged since the 17th century.

Because Farnham thrived as a commercial town, dealing in wheat and hops, it had a range of storage and processing buildings behind the business premises fronting the main streets. Yards and lanes, each sufficiently long to accommodate a wagon train, were used to service these premises. It is this network of backwaters – narrow lanes, passages and yards – set in complete contrast to the elegant Georgian street façades, which plays a large part in creating the special character of the town. Nowhere is this more evident than in Lion and Lamb Yard: it is space with both dynamic and static qualities which seems to have immense appeal to the people of Farnham. Careful detailing of the floorscape, the use of local materials and building styles, an articulation of the façades and the introduction of sculpture all contribute to a feeling of a place that is both familiar and suited to contemporary use.

LOCATION Lion and Lamb Yard is on the north side of West Street. Rail services from Waterloo. By road M3 then A325 or A287
LOCAL AUTHORITY Waverley Borough Council

Lyons+Sleeman+Hoare Architects

HASTINGS: TOWN CENTRE

During the 1990s Hastings was split by controversial proposals to close Priory Meadow – a county cricket ground – and introduce a major new shopping centre also to be known as Priory Meadow. Since its development, designed by Chapman Taylor Partners, controversy has continued but at the same time the development has become part of the town centre and improvements to Hastings Old Town together with pedestrianisation of the Victorian town centre have gone some way to relieve the impact of the new shopping centre. Success has only been partial. The combination of the three elements has, however, established a series of urban experiences that are worth exploring. Hastings Old Town sits huddled between the steep hills of the downs and the beach with its unique three-storey net-lofts and the narrow streets typical of many seaside towns. Of special note is the pocket park, Butlers Gap, that has been introduced through the combined efforts of the local community, the council and the private sector.

The route to the town centre leads west past one of the great opportunities in the town – the sadly neglected Regency crescent containing St Mary-in-the-Castle. An underpass with mosaic features leads gateway-like into the town centre. A piazza has been created and although total pedestrianisation has not been possible, café tables spread into Havelock Road and an intriguing lane leads to the much-criticised Priory Meadow. Even here, Queen's Square provides a place to sit and watch the world go by. The idiosyncratic towers of the centre provide new signposts leading the visitor back away from the seafront. Yes, there were lost opportunities but with the passage of time this cuckoo has become an interesting feature in the general townscape.

LOCATION the station is north of the town centre. Off street parking in the town centre.
LOCAL AUTHORITY Hastings Borough Council

pedestrianisation East Sussex County Council and Hastings Borough Council

HORSHAM: CARFAX AND WEST STREET

For many years Horsham was known as a rather scruffy market town beset by traffic congestion; 1960s' ring roads and 1970s' shopping and office insertions seemed merely to accentuate this image. Now thoughtful townscape design has transformed the centre of Horsham into a pleasing and lively urban place. In a bold step the district council closed West Street, a shopping street, to traffic. This was part of a plan to give a new identity to the whole town centre. Perhaps the most significant part of this plan was to create a new wholly pedestrian area based around Carfax into which a fanciful bandstand has been inserted. From Carfax radiate a number of alleyways, a remnant of the ancient heart of the town. Colletts Alley and Crown Alley both lead south to Middle Street and thus to West Street. At its western end is a new feature, the notorious Shelley Fountain. Installed at considerable expense to celebrate the poet Shelley, this sculptural fountain lifts its bronze sphere heavenward on a column of water every few moments. It's a pity that the buildings surrounding the space do not reflect the quality of effort that has clearly been put into the floorscape and sculpture. The prosaic Swan Walk with its standard shops leads back via Swan Square into Carfax with its trees and idiosyncratic street furniture.

Nearby is Crawley New Town, the second of Britain's first generation of new towns, showing signs of its age.

LOCATION from the station, Carfax is west down North Street; by car A264 from the M23, ample town-centre carparks
LOCAL AUTHORITY Horsham District Council

Horsham District Council

NEW ASH GREEN: VILLAGE CENTRE

New Ash Green is one of the most interesting and unconventional housing developments of the 1960s. Conceived by Span (Developments) Ltd, the vision was for a self-contained community with housing, industry, schools and a local centre, all for a large village of 4000 homes. It is set in rolling Kent countryside and the landscaping within the scheme was designed for a high-level of responsibility for maintenance from residents – an objective that has not been entirely achieved in the centre. Completed in the mid 1980s, the village covers 174 hectares of which 65 hectares is public open space. The village centre contains some 35 shops, a health surgery, office, studios and workshops, junior and secondary schools, a library and restaurants. The mainly three-storey village centre provides a vehicle-free shopping street with an informal grouping of buildings, some including arcades.

The architecture of New Ash Green is among the best of 1960s domestic design. it uses a limited palette of local yellow stock bricks, artificial slates and stained boarding and cladding. The layout is unusual, not least for its sense of very low density with segregated vehicular circulation and a network of pedestrian routes.

Nearby are Rochester, approximately 19 kilometres east; Gravesend 9.5 kilometres north-east; and Bluewater, the monster shopping centre, 9.5 kilometres north.

SOUTH-EAST ENGLAND

LOCATION rail station Longfield, 3 kilometres north. By car the A2 then A227 south, New Ash Green is signposted to the west. Persistence is needed
LOCAL AUTHORITY Sevenoaks District Council

Eric Lyons, Cunningham and Partners

WHITSTABLE: FISHERMEN'S BUILDINGS

Whitstable Harbour is compact and accessible, with a relaxed and friendly atmosphere and a bracing climate. During the last 25 years the harbour has been enhanced by the introduction of groups of elegant unaffected black painted and stained timber fishermen's buildings, integrated with the existing small-scale buildings of the harbour. These gable-ended working houses were designed with external timber staircases and balcony access. They can double-up as fishermen's stores, holiday accommodation and warehousing. Their scale is just right and they have added character and vitality. Whitstable must have one of the longest high streets of any small seaside resort in south-east England, but the harbour is definitely its focal point and it is close to the station and carparks.

Whitstable has a pleasantly laid-back feel with a good variety of shops, the famous Wheeler's Oyster Bar, known for its cosy atmosphere and good value, and both a museum and a castle. Canterbury and its cathedral are 11 kilometres to south on the A250; the historic town of Faversham is 18 kilometres west on the A299.

LOCATION from the station, take Railway Avenue 50 metres west then Cromwell Road north to the harbour. By car use the A299 but parking is limited
LOCAL AUTHORITY Canterbury City Council

Canterbury City Council

EASTERN ENGLAND

INTRODUCTION 3.2

BASILDON: NOAK BRIDGE 3.4

CAMBRIDGE: QUAYSIDE 3.6

CHELMSFORD: HIGH STREET 3.8

COLCHESTER: CULVER SQUARE 3.10

FAKENHAM: MARKET PLACE 3.12

HERTFORD: PARLIAMENT SQUARE 3.14

SOUTH WOODHAM FERRERS: TOWN CENTRE 3.16

NORWICH: ELM HILL 3.18

INTRODUCTION

The counties of Essex, Suffolk, Norfolk, Cambridgeshire and Hertfordshire comprise this region, one of wide open agricultural landscapes punctuated by the spire of a distant church or cathedral. It is the region of Constable and the 18th-century watercolourists. There are few major urban centres except on the southern edge close to London and on the coast at Harwich, Felixstowe and Ipswich. This is a region of brick and timber buildings. Lavenham, Thaxted and Saffron Walden are fine examples of the quiet domestic townscape these materials can generate.

The village architecture of the region is exemplified by Finchingfield with its pond, green and tumble of houses cascading from its village church. Such villages were the source of inspiration for a new vernacular form of domestic architecture promoted by Essex County Council's Design Guide and illustrated by Basildon's Noak Bridge (page 3.4).

Although much of the region is perceived as remote, London's housing pressures have made their mark and it contains seven of the country's new towns. Letchworth, home of the Garden City movement, is in the north of Hertfordshire; Stevenage, Welwyn Garden City, Hatfield and Hemel Hempstead lie closer to London. Each contains notable experiments in urban design but time has not treated them well and a process of regeneration and redevelopment has started in the centres of most of these new towns. It will be interesting to see if they emerge as good places. In Essex Frederick Gibberd, one of the pioneers of urban design, oversaw the creation of Harlow New Town which encompassed the original Harlow Old Town and is undergoing a similar process of regeneration.

South Essex is the most populous and industrialised part of the region. Basildon New Town and South Woodham Ferrers are public-sector-promoted attempts to provide a controlled outlet for growth. The low coastline provides the setting for some of England's oldest settlements. Colchester (page 3.10) is claimed to be 'Britain's oldest recorded town'. Its town walls remain in part and the small alleyways form much of the old town. Maldon and the much larger Ipswich are ancient ports. Maldon, with its unique triangular church tower, retains the character of a fishing port. Ipswich is a bustling port but its heart is based on a medieval street pattern. It has fine examples of the craft of pargeting (carved plasterwork), but also distinguished modernism with Norman Foster's Willis Faber Building the forerunner to many mirror-glass-clad office blocks. Market Place is undergoing revival and is a potential good place. In the north of the region, the Customs House of 1683 dominates the quay of King's Lynn, and there is new work in King's Staithe.

Pevsner says that Norwich has everything. There is a castle and a cathedral but notable among urban places is the market place next to the City Hall by James and Pearce (1938). Across the river Wensum, Magdalen Street was in 1959 the Civic Trust's first street redecoration scheme. The adjacent Colegate area shows a sensitive blend of old and new. A recent addition to the city is the new Library and Millennium Centre by Michael Hopkins. Outside Norwich on the Earlham Road is the University of East Anglia, masterplanned by Denys Lasdun, with the Sainsbury Centre by Norman Foster and student accommodation by Rick Mather combining to create a quasi-urban form.

Cambridge is the epitome of a university city, rivalling Oxford. Its courtyard-focussed colleges range in date from Clare College of 1326 to Robinson College of 1980. Architectural and townscape delights abound but what better way to end a tour of East Anglia than on the green banks of the Cam watching the punts drift under King's Bridge while a choir sings in nearby King's College Chapel (1466)?

BASILDON: NOAK BRIDGE

In the early 1970s Noak Bridge was the last phase of Basildon New Town to be built. It marked a departure from the design of the rest of the town and is generally regarded as one of the best late-20th-century housing developments in Essex. Separated from the rest of the town by the A127, Noak Bridge presented the opportunity to create a self-contained village based on local vernacular architecture and laid out on the principles set down in the Essex Design Guide. The well-treed site on the edge of the greenbelt site was attractive and insulated from the A127 by an anti-noise bund. Enormous variety was created, using 32 house types, flats and sheltered units, and a wealth of varied detail. The layout is apparently simple, but by using a sinuous alignment and varying width, it yields an unfolding sequence of views. Shared driveways give access to the rear of back gardens for most parking. Flats are used to turn corners.

The first phase of Noak Bridge became the most popular rented neighbourhood in Basildon. The contractors then asked the architects to design a second phase of housing for sale. Grafted seamlessly on to the first phase, this area has a slightly lower density. Its more fanciful architecture, and the way in which the roads and houses are woven in among retained trees, hedgerows and ponds, create places of great individuality. Noak Bridge focuses on a well-wooded public open space, corner shops, primary school and community hall. Further phases, built by other developers, are not as distinguished as the first.

LOCATION by bus from Basildon station or by car from the Billericay exit of the A127
LOCAL AUTHORITY Basildon District Council

Basildon Development Corporation

CAMBRIDGE: QUAYSIDE

Quayside is probably the most changed space in Cambridge, a truly magical site. The historic centre, it is now the conjunction of town and gown. A point of restricted vehicular movement, river traffic and pedestrian routes, the latter were transformed in the 1980s by the construction of a walk cantilevered from the buildings lining the river. This link is the most significant 20th-century improvement of public access in the city, reclaiming the river and redressing centuries of encroachment by colleges and university. The setting was so disregarded that in the 1980s it was said that '...Quayside cannot seriously claim to be a major part of the city...'. The redevelopment of 1984–90 enlarges the space by forming a three-sided court open to the river. The riverside is practically taken up by bars, cafés and restaurants animating the space. The orientation is crucial to its public success, which both tourists and Cambridge citizens can enjoy. On a hot day there are bicycles and punts and the animation of riverside activity. It is a place from which to take a punt tour or just watch and forms a lively setting for the offices surrounding the quay. The development provides links to Half Moon Court and Thompsons Lane and these links are another reason for the place's success. The architecture is not exciting but the variety of treatment and scale relates to Bridge Street and at the same time provides an enclosure which frames and shapes this outstanding enhancement.

All of central Cambridge is a joy, with high-quality buildings of all ages and sophisticated examples of traffic calming.

LOCATION Quayside is on the north-eastern side of Magdalene Bridge. Parking is very restricted. Cambridge station is south of the town centre
LOCAL AUTHORITY Cambridge City Council

Nicholas Ray Associates

CHELMSFORD: HIGH STREET

Chelmsford is the county town of Essex. Its High Street was originally the route leading north from the river crossing and was laid out with a triangular market place, later infilled. It is the focus of the town, and was remodelled in 1992. It focuses on John Johnson's Shire Hall of 1791 and is lined by a number of buildings dating from about 1800. In 1992 traffic was excluded from the High Street and it was repaved in yellow brick. This coincided with the opening of The Meadows, a covered shopping centre at the south end of the High Street which balances the existing Chelmer Precinct off the northern end. This portion of the High Street, which is somewhat wider, is fronted by two department stores and trees and reconstructed stone benches have been introduced. A decorative town sign on the site of a former conduit acts as a focus, and pedestrians are encouraged to linger. Paradoxically, the street furniture and trees work against the wish of the town manager to organise events to attract more people to the High Street.

LOCATION the station is up Duke's Street. Chelmsford is off the A12. The High Street is easily reached by bus and on foot, and there is plenty of parking
LOCAL AUTHORITY Chelmsford Borough Council

Chelmsford Borough Council

COLCHESTER: CULVER SQUARE

Culver Square is a new retail square formed in 1987 within the historic street pattern of Colchester's centre and is a unique addition to the open-air civic spaces of the town. The square, carefully located to form a focus at the western end of the town centre, is linked to Culver Street West and Sir Isaac's Walk. The liveliness of the square is ensured by 'anchor' stores in opposite corners. The buildings are two or three storeys high, in keeping with neaby building heights, and the major department store rises considerably higher. There is a good proportional relationship between the width of the square and the height of its enclosing buildings, and most is sunlit for a good part of the day. The square focuses on a centrally placed fountain. The architecture is in the exaggerated postmodern style of the 1980s, and the variety of building forms serves to emphasise the identity of the square. The totally retail character of the development has resulted in a lack of places to stop and eat or drink in an otherwise inviting space, and the square is dead after the shops have closed – but at least it is not closed off after hours. The buildings are all serviced from the basement.

No historic buildings were lost in the development which was preceded by an archaeological dig during which the foundations of a number of medieval houses were found. Colchester claims to be Britain's oldest recorded town and parts of the Roman city walls remain.

LOCATION Colchester's station is south of Culver Street via Queen Street and Culver Street West. There are carparks in the town centre
LOCAL AUTHORITY Colchester District Council

Sheppard Robson

FAKENHAM: MARKET PLACE

An existing market place in an historic market town previously used outside market days for parking has been transformed into an attractive public space within which the war memorial is located. The Market Place becomes the heart of Fakenham not only on the traditional market days but on other days when the seating, lighting features and public art are clearly shown to enhance the space. A series of cast-iron plates forms part of the hard landscaping; they represent the town's historic links with the printing industry. A range of seats, litter bins and lighting fixtures have been specifically designed for Fakenham. Artists were involved in the development of the designs, showing how contemporary design can enliven a space.

While visiting this area it is well worth going to King's Lynn where an extensive programme of environmental improvements has been undertaken. The area adjacent to the Custom House, Purfleet Quay, is an attractive space and King's Staithe Square includes a new performance space. South Quay along the river Ouse includes shelters, redesigned street furniture and public art.

EASTERN ENGLAND

LOCATION centre of Fakenham close to St Peter and Paul's Church
LOCAL AUTHORITY North Norfolk District Council

North Norfolk District Council and artists including Simon Watkinson

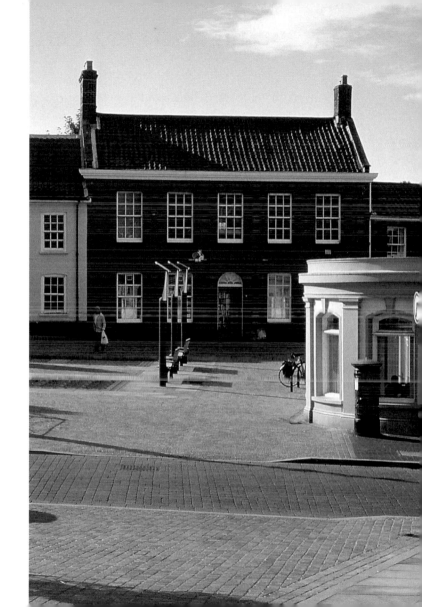

HERTFORD: PARLIAMENT SQUARE

Until March 1997, the centre of the small county town of Hertford was dominated by a traffic roundabout. All that changed with the introduction of the Parliament Square scheme. The square has always been of great townscape interest, with a pleasant mix of listed buildings – some formal, some vernacular – and there are some interesting shopfronts and displays around the three sides of the space. The focal point is the listed war memorial with its paved surroundings and life-size bronze sculpture of a hart. It is the newly pedestrianised paved area and café that have changed the feel of the space. Gone are the earlier traffic fumes. Now on a summer day the space is thronged with people just strolling or taking lunch or coffee at the open-air tables. In addition to Parliament Square, sections of Fore Street and Honey Lane together with parts of Market Place and Salisbury Square have been reclaimed for the pedestrian. High-quality materials and thoughtful tree planting have been used in combination with carefully selected street furniture to attract new users to the town centre.

Hertford lies midway between Welwyn Garden City and Hatfield New Towns to the west and Harlow New Town to the east.

LOCATION there are two stations: the North station is served from King's Cross, the East station from Liverpool Street. Hertford is on the A 414
LOCAL AUTHORITY East Hertfordshire District Council

East Hertfordshire District Council and Hertfordshire County Council

SOUTH WOODHAM FERRERS: TOWN CENTRE

South Woodham Ferrers town centre is a rare example of a late-20th-century greenfield town centre which is mixed-use, rather than shops fronted by parking.

The town is composed largely of houses for sale, laid out to Essex Design Guide principles between 1970 and 1990. The centre was to be an organic part of the town. Accordingly, the streets of the centre are continuations of pedestrian routes leading from all quarters of the town. The buildings have the same spans and pitches as the residential areas. To provide a centre early on it was necessary to attract a major food retail store and in 1977 Essex County Council held a competition. Tenderers were to provide mixed-use accommodation and the store. The winners, Asda, built a store, a square surrounded by shops, banks and workshop homes, plus the first section of a pedestrian street joining a complex of schools, library, community hall and church. One feature is a building with shops on the ground floor and temporary classrooms on the upper floors which can be converted to flats and offices when the school population declines. All buildings have shops on the street with flats and other uses above. Design briefs required that buildings fitted with their neighbours. The brick streets link three squares: in front of the store, in front of the school and church, and a market square. The streets are well enclosed, spaces vary in character and are well-used by pedestrians. Evening activity is generated by pubs, clubs, restaurants and sports facilities. There would have been more pedestrian movement had Asda not insisted on the major carpark being next to its store.

EASTERN ENGLAND

LOCATION South Woodham Ferrers can be reached by half-hourly bus from Chelmsford. By car take the A130 off the A127
LOCAL AUTHORITY Chelmsford Borough Council

Holder Mathias and Essex County Council

NORWICH: ELM HILL

This is not a 'place' in the conventional sense but a series of carefully contrived spaces linked by the river Wensum that passes between them. In the 1920s, Elm Hill, with its medieval, narrow, curving, cobbled streets, was semi-derelict, masking outdated slum and industrial property that faced similar near dereliction on the opposite side of the river. The Corporation decided to keep the property facing Elm Hill and to improve the area behind with a garden and riverside planting, a 1927 precursor of the Conservation Area of the Civic Amenities Act. It is now arguably the prime tourist attraction among Norwich streets. In the late 1960s the declining industrial area opposite, between the Wensum and Colegate, was purchased for residential development and in the early 1970s became the site of Friars Quay, a prize-winning townhouse scheme designed by Feilden & Mawson. In brick and tile, it responds to the spaces and the mature planting behind Elm Hill. Colegate itself has a number of old houses and churches and marks the boundary of the development.

Norwich has a castle, cathedral, the largest market square in Britain, and the new Forum development opposite the church of St Peter Mancroft. London Street was England's first pedestrianised street. Worth a detour is the campus of the University of East Anglia which includes the Sainsbury Centre for the Visual Arts.

EASTERN ENGLAND

LOCATION Norwich station is to the south east of Elm Hill and is reached by Prince of Wales Road, King Street and Wensum Street
LOCAL AUTHORITY Norwich City Council

Feilden & Mawson Architects

SOUTHERN ENGLAND

INTRODUCTION 4.2

FAREHAM: WEST STREET 4.4

MILTON KEYNES: QUEEN'S SQUARE 4.6

MILTON KEYNES: THEATRE SQUARE 4.8

OXFORD: GLOUCESTER GREEN 4.10

PORTSMOUTH: GUN WHARF QUAYS 4.12

PORTSMOUTH: OLD TOWN 4.14

READING: ORACLE CENTRE 4.16

WINCHESTER: HIGH STREET 4.18

WINDSOR: CENTRAL STATION 4.20

INTRODUCTION

Buckinghamshire, Oxfordshire, Berkshire, Hampshire and the Isle of Wight are included in this region. Many of the areas are on the line of the A34 linking the Midlands to the south-coast ports. The historic importance of the area stems from the roles of Oxford and Winchester in the academic and religious affairs of England. Oxford is the seat of the oldest English university (it awarded its first degrees in the 12th century)and the typology of the college quadrangle provides the basis for many urban-design ideas, including those of Leslie Martin. The High in Oxford is a perfect lesson in town building, its curvilinear form and its structures both of town and gown act together to provide what Thomas Sharp called 'a wonderfully rich and varied townscape'. The sequence of spaces running from The High through Radcliffe Square, with the circular Radcliffe Camera, into the Schools Courtyard and alongside the Sheldonian to Broad Street is a joy.

Also in Oxfordshire is Woodstock, which acts as a foil to the grandeur of Blenheim Palace; Witney, with a traditional market square, Church Green, and a well-thought-out addition to its shopping facilities; and Burford, 'the gateway to the Cotswolds', where the fine High Street slopes down to the river Windrush.

Buckinghamshire's county town is Aylesbury where the county council's multi-storey offices dominate a pleasantly pedestrianised centre. Milton Keynes (pages 4.6 and 4.8) is the major area of growth in the region. The new city centre provides regional shopping and leisure facilities, including a theatre. Within the overall development framework, Stony Stratford, an old coaching town, is worth visiting, as are Willen and Great Linford which now accommodate new development and their original communities. Contrasting with the new city there is the country house and estate of Woburn and the impressive landscape of Stowe.

Much of Berkshire is related to the river Thames. Attractive towns such as Windsor (page 4.20), Maidenhead, Cookham, Marlow and Henley take advantage of their riverside location. Further west, Newbury also uses its river and canal to provide a lung in the centre of the town overlooked by cafés and restaurants. Bracknell, one of the Mark I new towns, is set within a treed landscape.

Winchester, the capital of both Saxon and Norman England, is marked by its castle at the summit of the High Street and its cathedral and close at its lower end. The 13th-century great hall of the castle is now part of the modern crown court. Hampshire County Architects were responsible for the County Records Office near the railway station. The High Street, now pedestrianised, has examples of domestic buildings from all periods and the numerous small alleyways (twittens) leading from it are worth exploring.

Portsmouth (page 4.12) and Southampton are both ports dating from the Roman period. Both were extensively damaged in World War II and by the decline of Britain's maritime industry. Portsmouth is perhaps leading in regeneration, propelled by the realisation of the importance of the city's naval heritage, still to be fully realised in the historic dockyard, home to HMS 'Victory'. Less fortunate has been Portsmouth's twin town of Gosport, where work is progressing on Gosport's Millennium Walk along the harbour edge.

Southampton has recently undergone a major restructuring of its retailing through redevelopment of West Quay. Despite the existence of significant sections of its ancient city walls, a fine neoclassical civic centre and a superb location overlooking Southampton Water, its full potential has yet to be developed. Across Southampton Water is the New Forest. Within this area of outstanding natural beauty is Bucklers Hard – a tiny but complete Georgian shipbuilding village leading down to the Beaulieu river and the Solent. Further along the Solent is the charming port of Lymington, an attractive point of access to the Isle of Wight.

FAREHAM: WEST STREET

Public and private interests joined together in the Fareham Partnership to promote and develop a Millennium project that would mark the occasion with a permanent reminder of the area's historic past combined with improvements for the community. It was decided to revitalise the existing pedestrianised shopping area of West Street and, as part of that, to celebrate the life of Henry Cort who developed new methods of making wrought iron in the late 18th century. The street is used as the location for examples of blacksmith art and a series of outstanding sculptures are sited along it including entrance markers, water features and seating. A European-wide competition was used to obtain possible designs for the theme of 'The Market Place' and more than a hundred artists submitted proposals – 11 were chosen to produce work. A new shopping and leisure development is due to be constructed on the area to the south of West Street and a multi-use civic space has been provided – a focal point in the existing street, this will be enhanced by the future development. A circular performance podium provides a venue for concerts and school events and is also used as part of the market area. The Fareham Partnership worked with a wide range of agencies, civic societies and schools and the Millennium Commission, who grant-aided the project, to discuss and develop the concept.

West Street is an outstanding example of the integration of public art into a shopping area unified by an excellent hard landscape scheme. Completion of the adjacent Market Quay development should provide an enhanced community focus for the whole town centre.

LOCATION rail from Victoria and London Bridge; town centre signposted from junction 10 on M27. Several public carparks
LOCAL AUTHORITY Fareham Borough Council

design co-ordination Building Design Partnership (BDP)

MILTON KEYNES: QUEEN'S SQUARE

Queen's Square provides an oasis of outdoor space within the enclosed central shopping building, 'thecentre:mk'. Milton Keynes city centre provides a range of public spaces beginning with the often windswept Station Square outside the railway station. Three boulevards structure the city centre running east–west to connect into Campbell Park. The shopping building located between Midsummer and Silbury Boulevards contains two public spaces, one covered and one – Queen's Square – open-air. While the shopping centre is now regrettably closed outside shopping hours, Queen's Square provides an attractive and popular counterpoint to the enclosed Shopping Building, enhanced by its large pool of water, fountains, sculpture, pergola and cafés.

In *The Architecture and Planning of Milton Keynes* (1982), Derek Walker (chief architect of Milton Keynes Development Corporation from 1971 to 1976) emphasised the importance of designing the spaces between buildings. Traditionally '...a city's pride was in its squares, arcades, parks and boulevards, to which buildings added a complement. Milton Keynes, in this perspective, returns to this urban tradition by making infrastructure a positive contribution. In the central areas in particular, for the first time for many years, as much energy is being spent on the design of streets, boulevards and the spaces between buildings, as on the buildings themselves.'

A southern extension to the Shopping Building is provided by a light and airy link at Midsummer Place. A circular space, Oak Court, formed around a mature oak tree, leads to additional shopping space.

LOCATION Midsummer Boulevard is the central street running east from the station. 800 metres to the east is thecentre:mk

LOCAL AUTHORITY Milton Keynes Council

Milton Keynes Development Corporation

MILTON KEYNES: THEATRE SQUARE

A place has been created between the new theatre, central art gallery and restaurant providing the opportunity for interaction between the separate uses. The small public space forms part of the new theatre complex on Midsummer Boulevard. The theatre is more than an important cultural building – it also provides a place for people to gather and enjoy outdoor entertainment in a space defined by the separate small art gallery on one side and a restaurant on the other. The three separate elements are linked by a high-level canopy which enables the space to be given a specific definition and to be enhanced by lighting.

It is interesting to note that this development, given substantial lottery support, represents the first significant scheme to be implemented in central Milton Keynes since the development corporation was wound up by the government in 1992. The recent extension to the Shopping Building was the first development to break the mould of the masterplan but Theatre Square was undertaken within the structure rather than as part of the original masterplan. Its successful integration illustrates how a robustly prepared masterplan can act as a framework for innovation and not as a straitjacket into which developments must be shoe-horned.

SOUTHERN ENGLAND

LOCATION south side of Midsummer Boulevard opposite the end of thecentre:mk closest to Campbell Park
LOCAL AUTHORITY Milton Keynes Council

Andrzej Blonski and Michael Heard Architects

OXFORD: GLOUCESTER GREEN

A pleasant pedestrian square used as an open market and surrounded by mixed-use buildings containing shops, restaurants, an arts centre and flats. The square is used as a marketplace two days a week. This was one reason for requiring this area of open space in the city council's design brief; another was the general lack of such amenities in the central area. Trees define the central market space and the occasional servicing route which runs in front of the shops and the Old Fire Station, now an arts centre. The adjacent long-distance bus station is tightly planned to allow a further area of open space to be provided in front of the old school building, a listed arts-and-crafts-period building, designed by Leonard Stokes, which is now used as a pub. A public carpark is provided at basement level. Externally, the buildings derive inspiration from the arts-and-crafts period although it can be argued that they are related to surrounding buildings. On the south side of the square an existing cinema presents a blank façade to the space but this has been partially relieved by the location of kiosks.

LOCATION north-west part of the city centre between George Street and Beaumont Street, east of Worcester Street
LOCAL AUTHORITY Oxford City Council

Kendrick Associates

PORTSMOUTH: GUN WHARF QUAYS

In common with most of Britain's naval dockyards, Portsmouth Docks have been undergoing a period of decline and closure. Reuse of these large strategic sites has been both urgent and controversial. The Gun Wharf Quays, to the south of the Historic Dockyard and north of the Old Town (page 4.14) were closed in 1986. Designated a conservation area in 1996, at the same time Portsmouth City Council, the local planning authority, issued a planning brief. The proposal that the redevelopment should contain a large element of retail was the cause of considerable concern to the traders in Portsmouth's existing shopping area not far to the east. The case for a mixed-use scheme was irrefutable and in 1997 consent for redevelopment was issued.

Key features of the location are its waterfront setting and the historic Vernon and Vulcan buildings. The scheme prepared for The Berkeley Group places a range of bars, restaurants and pubs along a new City Quay. This promenade-like frontage overlooks a new marina and the busy waters of Portsmouth Harbour. Forming a link between the quay and the landward entrance is a sequence of retail squares intended also for use as ad-hoc performance venues and temporary exhibitions. The stone-floored Vulcan Building has been converted to residential and commercial uses and the former Customs House, the Vernon Building, has been converted into a pub. Unfortunately, security considerations have been allowed to override 24-hour living, but opening hours are generous if only to allow the multiplex cinema to function.

LOCATION to the south of Portsmouth Harbour station and ferry terminal. There is extensive underground parking and road access is fairly simple if the M275 is used to its southern end and local signs followed

LOCAL AUTHORITY Portsmouth City Council

GRA (Geoffrey Reid Associates)

PORTSMOUTH: OLD TOWN

A visit to Portsmouth means leaving the comfortable folds of the South Downs and battling through the semi-urban dross of low-rise wasteland that fills the coastal fringe. Past the sheds and terraces of this old naval town and by what must be one of the worst pedestrian routes anywhere one finds Guildhall Square. This, if a little less sterile, might have formed a good place. Into Victoria Park, avoiding the historic docks, probably the most dreadful and user-unfriendly pieces of national heritage, and we are in a mixture of stranded curios, tourist temptations and developer vernacular. This fascinating blend of water and history, sailmakers and fishing, pubs, tearooms, and housing makes King James Quay and its surroundings an exciting place. Contrast the twee Broad Street with its Sallyport Tea Rooms and Fortitude Cottage with the busy ferries, chaotic fishing boats and yachts that dreams are made of. Take a drink in the Spice Island Inn and enjoy the views over the harbour to the historic dockyard and the renaissance of Gun Wharf Quays. Newly installed sculptured seating allows the busy maritime scene to be enjoyed and this unique blend of old, new, workaday and fantasy to be seen as a good place in spite of doubts about the architectural style of recent additions.

SOUTHERN ENGLAND

LOCATION Portsmouth Harbour station is to the north of the Old Town and a short walk along Gunwharf Road. By road, take the A27 and A3 to the town centre
LOCAL AUTHORITY Portsmouth City Council

Portsmouth City Council

READING: ORACLE CENTRE

This development includes the river Kennet which flows between the Oracle Shopping Centre and its separate carpark. The Riverside is one of the most striking elements of the Oracle with its attractive promenade and a venue offering alfresco dining, live entertainment, a multiscreen cinema and the space to sit, read or just watch the world go by. The Riverside houses a variety of restaurants, cafés and bars and also includes a wide range of entertainment. The performance area is located alongside the river, highlighted by an expressive canopy, with the restaurants and cinemas linked across the river by a welcoming bridge.

Broad Street, the town centre's major street, is located on the north side of the Oracle Centre. This was pedestrianised in 1992 and a major streetscape project has recently been completed. The street was completely repaved with setts marking out delivery routes. Seating and tree planting are complemented by specially designed lighting columns, based on the old tramways traction-pole design – the whole design seeks to make historical links in order to enhance the sense of place. A forum area in the middle of the street with a raised circular plinth is designed to make good Reading's lack of a town square.

LOCATION the Oracle Centre is on the southern side of the town centre directly accessible from the Inner Distributor Road. Broad Street provides access to the Oracle Centre on its north-east side

LOCAL AUTHORITY Reading Borough Council

Haskoll & Co Ltd Architects

WINCHESTER: HIGH STREET

Winchester is one of England's oldest cities and home to King Arthur's fabled round table. Today's functional demands have required changes that have been handled with sensitivity and care. The structure of the core is simple and its new pedestrian area climbs from the river Itchen via the Broadway to the fully pedestrianised High Street, then up past the law courts to the Castle Hall. The High Street, heart of the city's pedestrianisation, is showing some signs of wear. There has been work to improve the friction of the paving, especially important on a sloping and often shady surface. The pubs in the side streets provide good places for a pint; Great Minster Street is a good place to see the careful road detailing. Lower down the High Street, Silver Hill leads north to a street market and to the Brooks shopping centre. Unfortunately this interesting insertion into the city is closed at night. At the top of the High Street is Walcote Place where new shops have been sensitively added and a new space created. Elizabeth Frink's *Man on Horseback* can be seen across the roadway.

Up the hill, the Castle Hall and law courts complex is worth a detour. A fine new County Records Office is just off the top of the High Street in Sussex Street. The cathedral dates from Saxon times.

LOCATION station is north of High Street off Jewry Street and City Road. Winchester is off the M3. There is a park-and-ride system
LOCAL AUTHORITY Winchester City Council

Hampshire County Council

WINDSOR: CENTRAL STATION

Windsor's Central Station has been a gateway to the town for millions of people. The quintessentially Victorian style and ornate detailing of the buildings were designed to welcome heads of state. They don't come to Windsor by train now, but the station welcomes increasing numbers of visitors from London. In the mid 1990s the economic potential of redeveloping the station and its environs was recognised. Retail units, cafés and restaurants could not fail to thrive from the passing tourists. The redeveloped station is, however, more than a retail addition to the town. It has created a public space which cleverly overcomes the town centre's distinct but difficult level changes and links Windsor's retail centre with the tourist-dominated castle and riverside area.

Until 1997 Windsor lacked a public space not under the ownership of the Crown. Now the 'back' of the town centre has been opened up, enhancing safety and security. This, combined with the successful pedestrianisation of Peascod Street to the south, has quite changed the character of the town. An emphasis on quality materials has created a number of attractive spaces under the original glass roof of the station allowing 'people watching' to take place in any weather. Events are arranged and it is rare to visit the station without hearing live music. The shops and cafés may not be to everyone's taste (or budget) but they help to radiate an up-market atmosphere. You can't help but feel good even if you're just passing through.

Windsor Castle can hardly be avoided and it does contain a notable art collection and some fine medieval architecture.

LOCATION Windsor Station is served by London's Paddington and is close to the M4 motorway

LOCAL AUTHORITY Royal Borough of Windsor and Maidenhead

Diamond Lock Grabowski

SOUTH-WEST ENGLAND AND SOUTH WALES

INTRODUCTION 5.2
BOURNEMOUTH: THE SQUARE 5.4
BRISTOL: ST AUGUSTINE'S REACH 5.6
BRISTOL: MILLENNIUM SQUARE 5.8
CARDIFF: WATERFRONT 5.10
CHELTENHAM: THE COURTYARD 5.12
DORCHESTER: POUNDBURY 5.14
EXETER: QUAYSIDE 5.16
FROME: THE PIGGERIES 5.18
GLOUCESTER: THE DOCKS 5.20
NEWTON ABBOT: COURTENAY STREET 5.22
PLYMOUTH: THE BARBICAN 5.24
SWANSEA: MARITIME QUARTER 5.26
SWANSEA: WIND STREET 5.28
TEIGNMOUTH: THE TRIANGLES 5.30

INTRODUCTION

The south-west region includes the counties of Dorset, Somerset, Wiltshire, Devon, Cornwall and Gloucestershire together with the 'good places' found in South Wales. The region features a variety of landscapes and urban forms. There is the high sophistication of Regency Bath with its set pieces – the Royal Crescent by John Wood the Younger, Queen's Square and the Circus by John Wood the Elder, Pulteney Bridge by Robert Adam. There are the maritime delights of the Cornish fishing villages of Mousehole and Polperro. None of these locations has produced new places for inclusion in this guide – perhaps it is impossible to improve on perfection. Wholly new places like Poundbury and regenerated places like Plymouth's Barbican add to the richness and diversity that make up the region.

Inclusion of South Wales and Gloucestershire in this region may seem unusual. However, if Bristol is considered as the focus then a coherent travel plan can be evolved covering most of the places. The most easterly, The Square in Bournemouth, reflects the resorts of the south-east, but the air is milder and the foliage richer. Inland the scenery is more dominantly rural than in areas closer to London. Housing pressures are numerically less but no less urgent. It is therefore interesting to see the Poundbury experiment at Dorchester.

Dorset, Somerset and Wiltshire have a wealth of small market towns, many of which are suffering from lack of investment. Developments currently underway in Calne, Devizes and Frome illustrate the fine quality of urban space that these towns can present. A remarkable example is Marlborough in Wiltshire with its wide High Street and Georgian façades. The region is rich in towns with an ecclesiastical foundation; outstanding are Salisbury, Wells, Glastonbury and Gloucester.

The potential for dockside and waterside developments to create opportunities for good places is illustrated by the number of examples in the guide. There are several other water-related towns that have potential, particularly Weymouth, Poole and Totnes, a British Council of Archaeology 'gem town' whose High Street is a delight in a town of awful suburbs. Cornwall's Atlantic coast provides particular charms, nowhere more so than at St Ives where the redevelopment of an old gasworks has provided a striking setting for one of Britain's most modern galleries, the Tate Gallery St Ives (designed by Evans & Shalev). Near St Austell the Eden Project (by Nicholas Grimshaw) brings the tropics to abandoned clay workings.

In Bristol, Millennium Square provides a new focus to the lower part of the city, but the College Green and Clifton with its elegant 18th-century Windsor Terrace, Cornwallis Crescent, Royal York Crescent, Paragon and suspension bridge by Brunel are worth a visit. To the north of Bristol is the village of Blaize Hamlet designed by John Nash in 1811 to house estate pensioners, an early planned settlement?

The south coast of Wales was host to some of the most highly industrialised area of Britain and the ports of Cardiff and Swansea were once among the busiest in Europe. In common with most ports in the UK, maritime trade here has diminished and an urban development corporation or a progressive city council have sought to regenerate the city's fortunes. In Cardiff much of quality still remains , including the Arcades and Cathays Park. Inland, ancient Chepstow and Monmouth typify the border towns. Recently Caerphilly has remodelled its town centre as part of a regeneration programme and is worth a detour.

BOURNEMOUTH: THE SQUARE

Bournemouth Square used to be a crowded traffic intersection dividing the shopping centre. Gradual changes have removed traffic and transformed it into a safe pedestrian space that unites the centre and creates a natural focal point. In keeping with the image of Bournemouth, the Square pays homage to the sun, being open to the south and forming a bright oasis between the shadowed streets. Towards the north a freestanding café (by Trinity Architects) with outside seating has been introduced in the middle of the space. It is circular, and its smaller first-floor houses a camera obscura. This extra height is vital to compete with the surrounding buildings whose style and gravitas confirm their town-centre location. The Square is a lively thoroughfare for pedestrians as they cross between the two shopping streets or perhaps stop at the café. Only buses and taxis now reach the Square and they are hidden by exotic landscaping and orientation. Materials and planting are high quality.

While uses are limited, the area is fast acquiring restaurants and night life that extend the vitality of the Square beyond shop closing. In Bournemouth Square, careful exclusion of traffic and the prudent introduction of the right uses have transcended the architecture and openness to form a lively new asset to the town. A good example of the combination of urban design and engineering.

LOCATION Bournemouth Square is at the junction of Commercial Road and Old Christchurch Road. The station is to the north up Lansdowne Road
LOCAL AUTHORITY Bournemouth Borough Council

landscape architects Gillespies

BRISTOL: ST AUGUSTINE'S REACH

Since John Cabot left from here to 'discover' the New World, St Augustine's Reach has been at the heart of Bristol's seafaring heritage. Today that same tongue of water laps at the centre of a modern city, creating a fusion of bustling activity, tranquillity, safety and surprise. A busy and noisy road at the north end has been replaced with a modern landscaped space. You can walk safely into the shopping area to the north and steps take you down to the water's edge. To the right is a continental colonnade and to the left a broad space with a line of trees; in the middle distance cranes and docks and, beyond, the Somerset countryside. Gone is the noise of traffic. Here are the smell of joss sticks, waterside coffee houses and flower sellers, all touched with the allure of glistening water. To the west of the Watershed new leisure buildings of spectacular architecture are grouped around a modern plaza. Walking through Watershed you can look back into the city or out over the water. At the south-west tip of the Reach a magnificent 360-degree view reveals the landmarks of the city.

Across the water, the Arnolfini Gallery commands the south-east end of the Reach. Outside, eaters and drinkers invite you over the new and splendidly flamboyant footbridge designed by Eilís O'Connell. There is a buzz at the Arnolfini; boats moor at the quay wall, knots of people throng the water's edge and there is always the expectation that something unusual could happen. And there's that view again.

LOCATION take Redcliffe Way from Templemeads station. The closest parking is in Prince Street
LOCAL AUTHORITY Bristol City Council

Alec French Partnership and Ferguson Mann Architects with Bristol City Council

BRISTOL: MILLENNIUM SQUARE

A new square has been created as part of the Canon's Marsh development scheme. It attracts many people and children, not just because of the surrounding uses but also because of the imaginative water feature.

A Harbourside Design Forum established principles for the development of the area and successful applications for funding were made by a new organisation, @t Bristol, to the Millennium Commission. The main components of @t Bristol are Explore, a new-generation interactive science centre; Wildscreen, a natural-history centre incorporating a tropical house and an IMAX cinema; and major new public spaces. A separate application, unfortunately unsuccessful, was made to the Arts Council to fund a centre for the performing arts including a concert hall and dance studio. An underground carpark serving all these uses is constructed below the public square.

The route from St Augustine's Wharf passes first through Anchor Square – where the entrance to Wildscreen, designed by Michael Hopkins, is located – and on to which a number of restaurants and bars front. The route then passes into Millennium Square where Explore with its exciting globe, designed by Wilkinson Eyre, forms the northern edge. Explore's café spills out into the square which is enlivened by a series of shallow pools, illuminated jets and a cascade. Water features were designed by William Pye and lighting elements by David Ward and Martin Richman.

LOCATION Canons Marsh, west of St Augustine's Wharf
LOCAL AUTHORITY Bristol City Council

Concept Planning Group (Alec French Partnership and Ferguson Mann Architects)

CARDIFF: WATERFRONT

The old harbour area had the world's second-highest tidal range with more than 16 metres difference between high and low water. With the loss of trade, harbour maintenance declined, and the mud-flats revealed when water levels were low became a feeding ground for migratory birds. In 1987 the Inner Harbour was identified as a prime location for regeneration and the old Pierhead Building, originally designed 'combining muscular Gothic and French Renaissance elements' by William Frame was perceived as the flagship building. The Inner Harbour was to be an arc of entertainment. There are now three leisure activities in the Inner Harbour: a hands-on science museum, Techniquest; a varied mix of restaurants and bars; and a visitor centre. Of interest are the converted Norwegian church, now a café/gallery, and Britannia Park, with sculpted furniture. Open-air concerts are often staged. Abandonment of the Welsh National Opera building designed by Zaha Hadid was a blow but preparations are proceeding on the Wales Millennium Centre and the National Assembly for Wales, both in the Inner Harbour.

With the Cardiff Bay Barrage, the mud flats and migratory birds have disappeared. However, the weather still generates spectacular and constantly changing skyscapes. The Inner Harbour provides varied waterfront spaces for visitors, with a sculpture of a couple with a dog which is patted so frequently that it has developed a shiny metallic surface. The Oval Basin, designed by Nicholas Hare Architects, provides an imaginative performance venue within the old harbour walls and is given an added dimension by spectacular lighting.

Cardiff's Cathays Park civic centre and the Arcades are also worth a visit.

LOCATION Cardiff's Central station is 1.5 kilometres north-west
LOCAL AUTHORITY Cardiff City Council

Cardiff Bay Development Corporation

CHELTENHAM: THE COURTYARD

Montpellier Street is a specialist shopping area to the west of the town centre and The Courtyard development is located on its north-west side. The Courtyard extended the form of an 1840s terrace by adding five bays in a three-storey pastiche style and then contrasting this with a glazed pavilion which has two storeys at street level and a storey below this, fronting on to a courtyard. Steps down from the street lead into this lower level space in which there are restaurants and shops. At first-floor level more shops and gallery uses are linked by a glazed arcade. Offices and flats occupy the upper floors of the enclosing L-shaped building. The whole development is sympathetic to the existing area but expresses itself in a new form of space in a somewhat postmodern style.

The Courtyard has tremendous potential as a setting for events such as music – which occurred in earlier years – and the introduction of more interesting planting. It needs to be seen within the context of the wider Montpellier area with the caryatids of Montpellier Walk close by. It is set within the Regency town with its terraces and open spaces – 'the essence of Cheltenham... is a bracing mix of open air, trees, grass and breezy vistas across wide pavements'.

The town received a Europa Nostra award for a decade of town regeneration, an example of which is the completion of Queen's Parade which replaced a carpark.

LOCATION Montpellier Street, to the west of Cheltenham town centre
LOCAL AUTHORITY Cheltenham District Council

Stanley Partnership Architects

DORCHESTER: POUNDBURY

The Duchy of Cornwall's development at Poundbury is considered by some to be one of the most influential pieces of urban design in Britain. Poundbury challenges the basis of most suburban development and applies a set of urban-design ideals to the creation of a new place. It reflects the compactness of traditional Dorset towns. Streets have continuous edges with no front gardens. Courtyards and alleys create a subtle network of spaces and routes. Landmark buildings act as markers and a variety of spaces is formed by the careful positioning of buildings along curving streets inviting you to walk around the next corner. The series of views, changing shapes and spaces provide a rich visual experience.

The street is public space in Poundbury. Cars are slowed, children play in parking courts overlooked by houses placed in the courtyards. On-street parking is encouraged. Spaces are calmed; the street recreated. The architecture is rich and varied (arguably too varied) and the use of local materials creates a warm, intimate environment. People used to older urban areas will be aware of the controlled feel of the development. So far, there remains an unreal comfortableness. Uses other than housing have been introduced but have not had a major impact. These are early days and the next five years of expansion will be critical. The masterplan for Poundbury was unveiled by Leon Krier in 1989 and the first phase started in 1994. Houses have been designed individually or in small groups by local architects.

LOCATION Poundbury is on the B3150, Bridport Road, about 1.5 kilometres west from Dorchester. Local bus service and stations at Dorchester
LOCAL AUTHORITY West Dorset District Council

masterplan Leon Krier

EXETER: QUAYSIDE

Exeter is an ancient city, but it suffered heavily from war-time damage. The Quayside has medieval origins, and the canal basin is 16th century. Until the 1970s it was surrounded by public housing and a boat museum. It was little used and a strategy was drawn up to link the sides by a pedestrian bridge and remove parking from the Quayside. New private housing on land owned by the city council was used to help fund the improvements. Briefs were drawn up and progressively implemented, bringing empty buildings back into use. Warehouses on the quayside were renovated by the Quay and Canal Trust for offices and a pub, and the old medieval wharf, discovered at this time, is now a visitor centre. Specialist shops have opened up in the ground floors of the old buildings. The suspension bridge encourages people to stroll around and watch what is happening on the water. The new housing is of the right scale for a waterfront and has stimulated the building of other developments. Around the quay today there are interesting examples of the adaptation of old buildings for new uses, the introduction of high-density housing and the provision of places to browse and drink in. The area is also lively at night.

LOCATION Exeter St David's station is north-west of the city. The quay is well signposted down the hill from the city centre and its fine multi-storey carpark
LOCAL AUTHORITY Exeter City Council

masterplan URBED with Niall Phillips Architects

FROME: THE PIGGERIES

Like many other rural towns, Frome is suffering decline. Many inhabitants commute to Bath and an out-of-town superstore has forced the closure of town-centre shops. The town, which sits in a steep narrow valley, has more than 300 listed buildings – English Heritage describe it as 'a jewel'. Between 1665 and 1725 it grew as a wool and cloth manufacturing centre, giving rise to of some of England's earliest industrial housing on a grid plan north of the town centre. The wool trade declined and with it the town and its housing, to such an extent that in the 1960s the housing area was identified as a route for an inner relief road, causing further blight.

In the 1980s Mendip District Council persuaded the county council to abandon its road proposals. The way was now clear for redevelopment and improvement of this part of town. Fragmented ownership inhibited land assembly but by 1995 the site was acquired. A project group, including housing and planning departments, highway engineers, housing associations and architects, was set up. Meetings with residents established key design principles which included the need for active street frontages and – contrary to police advice – the retention of cross-site footpaths. Completion in 1998 provided a community of 71 homes predominantly for rent but stylistically indistinguishable from other tenures. A variety of building heights link the scheme to adjoining areas yet create a feeling of enclosure within the housing. Retaining the footpaths allowed casual supervision and added vitality. Careful detailing means that bin stores, car bays and lighting are an integral part and not discordant additions.

LOCATION up Stoney Street from town centre, right into Catherine Hill and Catherine Street, left at the Sun public house and down to the Piggeries
LOCAL AUTHORITY Mendip District Council

The Architecture and Planning Group

GLOUCESTER: THE DOCKS

You will see, suddenly appearing, as if in a dream, long ranges of warehouses, with cranes attached, endless intricacies of docks, miles of tramroad, wildernesses of timber in stacks, and huge, three-masted ships, wedged into little canals, floating with no apparent means of propulsion, and without a sail to bless themselves with. (Charles Dickens)

Today, some of the warehouses have been restored to their former glory, in contrast to earlier calls for demolition. Gloucester City Council gave major support to the regeneration of the city's docks by imaginatively converting a number of the substantial warehouses for its own use. The three buildings directly on the waterfront, the Herbert, Kimberley and Philpott warehouses, designed by Stanley Partnership Architects, have been linked with steel and glass structures which cause minimal disturbance to those buildings. A pub and restaurant add waterside activity and an earlier glazed pavilion includes shopping and cafés. A further warehouse operates as an antiques centre and others house offices and a small museum.

The National Waterways Museum is located in the Llanthony warehouse and provides a unique experience with films and working models. Two quaysides with historic boats add colour to an attractive destination. It is perhaps surprising that little housing has been provided in the area but there are still sites that could provide opportunities.

LOCATION on south-west side of the city centre to the south of the cathedral. Accessible off the A40
LOCAL AUTHORITY Gloucester City Council

Stanley Partnership Architects

NEWTON ABBOT: COURTENAY STREET

Newton Abbot could be described as a railway town without the usual accompanying industrialisation. It is a flourishing market town with the legacy of its railway age, Italianate suburbs of genteel villas, scattered up the surrounding hills. At the end of Courtenay Street is St Leonard's Tower, part of a 14th–15th-century church that was demolished in 1836. This and the surrounding buildings can be viewed as the area's only quality townscape following the over-enthusiastic town planning of the mid 20th century. Yet Courtenay Street rises above the mediocre architecture. Is it that people are the dominant element, given space to pause, chat or just window-shop? Could it be the lush foliage that has transformed the street into an oasis, giving glimpses of buildings and vistas, while offering shade and a green lung right in the heart of the shopping centre?

The history of the town is represented in the detailing of the street surfacing, where Dartmoor granite roundels give a timeline of influential historical and social events associated with Newton Abbot. Isambard Kingdom Brunel brought his railway here in 1846. The Haytor Granite Tramway, opened in 1820, was used to transport granite from Dartmoor to repair London Bridge and for use in the building of the National Gallery. The historical links are also maintained in the reclaimed and restored gates that provide an entry feature to the street.

LOCATION 19 kilometres south of Exeter on the A380. Newton Abbot station is accessible from Exeter and Plymouth

LOCAL AUTHORITY Teignbridge District Council

Devon County Council and Teignbridge District Council

PLYMOUTH: THE BARBICAN

Every boy in England should be taken at least once to Plymouth. He should, if small, be torn away from his mother and sent out for a night with the fishing fleet; he should go out in the tenders to meet the Atlantic liners; he should be taken to the Barbican and told the story of the Mayflower and the birth of New England... (H V Morton, *In Search of England*, 1927)

The Barbican is a 'living-working' place with a strong local community. Home of Plymouth's fishing industry and a popular tourist area, its history makes it an important place locally and internationally – the 'Mayflower' departed for America from the Barbican Quay. The historic townscape is centred on Sutton Harbour. One of the first conservation areas to be designated (in 1967), it was awarded the status of 'outstanding conservation area' in 1977. An Elizabethan suburb to medieval Plymouth, it is characterised by its maritime setting, irregular 16th-century streets and variety of building styles. A mix of uses, among them housing, shops, galleries and cafés, make it an active place day and evening. Regeneration included infrastructure improvements. New visitor attractions include the National Marine Aquarium and a centre for Dartington Glass, good examples of 1990s architecture. Further enhancements will occur as part of the 'Life Around the Harbour' strategy, including a new visitor centre. Abercrombie's town centre on either side of Armada Way was a classic of post-war rebuilding and has been refurbished.

Jeremy Dixon's Sainsbury's supermarket at Marsh Mills and Nicholas Grimshaw's Western Morning News building at Derriford are worth a detour.

LOCATION south down Armada Way to Hoe Park, east along Citadel Road and Castle Street

LOCAL AUTHORITY Plymouth City Council

Plymouth City Council

SWANSEA: MARITIME QUARTER

The South Dock has been imaginatively redeveloped and reused for housing, a marina, a museum and restaurants and is notable for the integration of public art relating to the history of the area.

Opened in 1859 as a result of Swansea's importance as a copper-smelting centre, the South Dock eventually closed in 1969. The city council assembled the land for development and produced imaginative planning briefs for the disposal of individual sites. It also coordinated the hard landscaping and public art throughout the area, and ensured that there was continuous public access to the waterfront. The northern side of the dock includes three- and four-storey social housing and private residential development. Here the existing pumphouse and other structures have been reused for a restaurant and museum purposes. On the other side of the dock a deeper site has enabled a wider range of residential uses to be provided on Ferrara Quay, designed by Halliday Meecham Partnership. The southern side of this site overlooks Swansea Bay where a new promenade has been created. Along this promenade are a number of features such as a sea-gate and an observatory which reflects the history of the area and its navigational beacons. Much of the development adopts a postmodern design approach.

Throughout the development, key locational points have been used to refer to the history of the area and these have been designed or coordinated by Robin Campbell to create a unique connection with its heritage.

LOCATION on the west bank of the river Tawe south of the city centre; parking is available off Oystermouth Road
LOCAL AUTHORITY Swansea City Council

masterplan Swansea City Council, Planning Department

SWANSEA: WIND STREET

Located at the gateway to the city centre near the castle ruins (where a major open space has been provided close to pedestrianised Oxford Street), Wind Street shows what can be achieved by providing more pavement space for activities, adding trees, introducing public art to enhance street furniture and using good-quality paving materials.

Wind Street is one of the last remaining historic streets of Swansea city centre following devastation in the war and slum clearance. URBED carried out a city-centre study and proposed that Wind Street should be improved to link the city centre with the regenerated waterfront.The sensitive environmental works that followed have successfully improved the qualities of the streetscape by focussing on the pedestrian environment while maintaining two-way traffic on what was the key city-centre spine from the High Street into the commercial district. The conservation-area streetscape combines valued 19th-century architecture with high-quality materials and planting to provide active street frontages and a safe and pleasant pedestrian environment. The street has now found a role as a vibrant café quarter and existing buildings have been recycled for new uses.

LOCATION Wind Street is a continuation of High Street and Castle Street and lies to the south and east of the main shopping centre
LOCAL AUTHORITY Swansea City Council

Swansea City Council Planning Department

TEIGNMOUTH: THE TRIANGLES

When is a triangle a square? When for the first time a town has a focus where people can meet, sit and chat, enjoy a leisurely drink at one of numerous street cafés or listen to a salsa band as part of a regular arts programme. Teignmouth, a traditional south Devon 'bucket-and-spade' resort with a working port, had experienced a spiral of decline. Today, a visitor who had last seen the town ten years ago would find an entirely different place: enhanced pedestrian-priority streets; a Lottery-funded decorative lighting scheme, plus a newly created town square, The Triangles.

The area had become choked with traffic and parked cars but the space now offers the opportunity to stroll and appreciate the listed 19th-century buildings flanking it. Among these is the Royal Library, a former publishing house from which the first Teignmouth guide was issued in 1817. The fine façade echoes the style adopted by many *cottages ornées* that dot the countryside around the town. Public art has played an important part in reinforcing the identity of the area, not 'add-ons' but fully integrated art incorporated into seats, bollards and other items of street furniture; a pedestrian barrier in the form of a fish screen where a curtain-net holds a catch of stylised bass, mackerel and other fruits of the sea. The practical has been combined with humour. The result is an area which people are proud both to be associated with and to own, confirmed by the sponsorship of seats by the local community and businesses.

LOCATION 19 kilometres south of Exeter and 10 kilometres north of Torquay on the A381. There is a local station
LOCAL AUTHORITY Teignbridge District Council

Devon County Council and Teignbridge District Council

THE MIDLANDS

INTRODUCTION 6.2
BIRMINGHAM: VICTORIA SQUARE 6.4
BIRMINGHAM: CHAMBERLAIN SQUARE 6.6
BIRMINGHAM: CENTENARY SQUARE 6.8
BIRMINGHAM: BRINDLEYPLACE SQUARE 6.10
BIRMINGHAM: GAS STREET BASIN 6.12
CHESTERFIELD: MARKET SQUARE 6.14
HEREFORD: LEFT BANK VILLAGE 6.16
LEICESTER: BEDE ISLAND NORTH 6.18
NOTTINGHAM: CASTLE WHARF 6.20
NOTTINGHAM: PLAYHOUSE SQUARE 6.22

INTRODUCTION

The Midlands region covers England from the Welsh border across to the North Sea. It contains the major urban centres of the Pottery Towns, the West Midlands Metropolitan Area and the East Midlands towns of Leicester and Nottingham, and continues as far north as Derby and Chesterfield. In the west the soft landscape of Herefordshire follows the river Severn into Shropshire and to Ludlow – one of Gordon Cullen's case studies in his seminal book *Townscape*. Shrewsbury, sited on what is almost an island in a bend of the Severn, is one of the best-preserved medieval towns in England and has used traffic-calming to its advantage. Shropshire also includes the new town of Telford, and Ironbridge, the cradle of the industrial revolution and a World Heritage Site.

In the West Midlands, regeneration initiatives can be seen in Wolverhampton, Walsall – with its innovative bus station and new art gallery – but particularly in Birmingham. When it sought to overcome the disadvantages of the concrete collar of its inner ring road, Birmingham became a principal example of urban design as a key planning issue. Five interlinked places (pages 6.4–6.12) are described below, and further work such as the Millennium Centre and Jewellery Quarter justify an extended visit. In Coventry there are exciting proposals which will help to restore the quality of the pioneering post-war city centre.

North of Birmingham is Lichfield, a small city with an attractive cathedral close, a charming cobbled market square and links with the lexicographer Dr Johnson. To the south is Warwick where one of England's finest castles dominates the townscape. Nearby is Royal Leamington Spa whose prefix is a sign of its attraction to Queen Victoria. Its dominant architectural styles are Regency and early Victorian. Of particular note are the set pieces of Lansdowne Crescent and Circus and the Parade. Further south is Stratford upon Avon with a Palladian town hall and a collection of timber-framed buildings.

North-east into Leicestershire across the M1 is Market Harborough with its triangular 'Square' and rejuvenated Union Wharf. Leicester itself (page 6.18) is a largely industrial city (but it was from here that Thomas Cook ran his first package tour). This is the home of two universities, both with notable engineering buildings: Leicester's by Stirling and Gowan and De Montfort's energy-conscious exemplar by Short Ford Associates.

Continuing north, J B Priestley claimed that Nottingham has a reputation for frivolity but it is the home to the Inland Revenue's new headquarters (by Michael Hopkins). Nottingham Castle dominates the southern part of the city and the Council House with its domed roof looms over the city centre. The medieval city lies under the more recent buildings of the Lace Market, an expression of Nottingham's industrial past. Another legacy of this is the Nottingham Canal which forms the setting for Castle Wharf (page 6.20). One of the city's architectural contributions to the last century is Nottingham Playhouse which Peter Moro completed in 1963. Recent work has made Playhouse Square an attractive new space (page 6.22). To the east the cathedral city of Lincoln stands out on a hilltop. The cathedral, the third largest in England, shares the site with the castle. Together they create one of England's great urban places. The medieval Steep Hill gives access to the lower town and the Strait. Further east, Louth, a small and complete country market town, provides a complete contrast to the drama of Lincoln. Its red brick and pantile buildings are grouped to form a series of overlapping spaces that add delight to urban living. Stamford, 80 kilometres south of Lincoln, which owed its medieval prosperity to the woollen trade, is described as having 'a sustained architectural dignity' which explains its frequent use for films. In Derbyshire, north of the larger East Midlands towns, Ashbourne's interesting marketplace, Buxton's Crescent and Chesterfield's rescued Market Square (page 6.14) offer urban attractions within the landscape of the Dales and Pennines.

BIRMINGHAM: VICTORIA SQUARE

The following five spaces (pages 6.4–6.12) are linked in a natural progression. There are three civic spaces that link to Birmingham's newest space, Brindleyplace Square, which also connects via the canal towpath to Gas Street Basin. Victoria Square is the closest to New Street Station, the point at which many visitors arrive in the city centre. Victoria Square plays a classical tune but it is an irregular city space dominated throughout its life by traffic, drawing attention away from the many fine listed buildings in eclectic Victorian styles: a council house in the style of a Venetian *palazzo*, a town hall (concert hall) which replicates a classical temple, a former post office modelled on a French chateau. The pedestrianisation of Victoria Square in 1993 was the flagship project of Birmingham's efforts to 'give the streets back to the people'. True to the city's confident Victorian past, all the shops were pulled out to remodel this steeply sloping site, creating a public space that matches the best in Europe. A huge fountain provides the centrepiece, cascading down the slope. Its location, centred on the axis of the council house façade with steps and stonework to either side, presents a dramatic composition with the flavour of the Spanish Steps in Rome, particularly when seen as you move up New Street.

Victoria Square is a truly great public place where historic buildings blend with confident landscaping and a busy pedestrian crossroads. If you believe we cannot create great city spaces in Britain, come here. If you cannot believe Birmingham can be an attractive city, come here. If you want to see the taciturn Brummies splash in a fountain, photographing each other as if on holiday in their own city, come here.

LOCATION from Birmingham New Street station turn east up New Street
LOCAL AUTHORITY Birmingham City Council

Landscape Practice Group, Birmingham City Council

BIRMINGHAM: CHAMBERLAIN SQUARE

Leaving Victoria Square on its north-western side you enter the smaller Chamberlain Square. This has its own role to play in Birmingham's cityscape. It climbs steeply from the fine Victorian buildings of the town hall and the council house to the concrete deck that carries the 1970s Central Library and School of Music over the Queensway. Its centre-piece, like all the best Birmingham squares, is another fountain, in this case the restored grand Victorian monument to Joseph Chamberlain and his 'civic gospel'. The steep south-facing steps below the library entrance make the square into an amphitheatre – a perfect way to fulfil its role as a 'speakers' corner', to accommodate street theatre, and another place to watch the world go by as they make their way by the curving ramp from the core of the city to Centenary Square and Broad Street beyond. Opposite, above the main entrance to the Museum and Art Gallery, the clock tower contains Big Brum, Birmingham's answer to Big Ben. Passing into the library, you enter an interior public space with cafés and shops. Leaving at the western end you enter Centenary Square.

There are proposals to redevelop the library site and it is important that the conti-nuity of spaces is maintained.

LOCATION from the east via Victoria Square; from the west via the Central Library
LOCAL AUTHORITY Birmingham City Council

John Madin Design Group

BIRMINGHAM: CENTENARY SQUARE

Centenary Square, laid out in 1991, is a large (perhaps too large) and very open (perhaps too open) space. In the 1930s it was intended to be a grand civic area with classical Portland stone buildings all around. In practice only the Hall of Memory, Baskerville House, the (former) Birmingham Municipal Bank and the (former) Masonic Temple were built to that vision. Birmingham's repertory theatre and the International Convention Centre, Symphony Hall and Hyatt Hotel have added culture and business. In front of the Convention Centre and the repertory theatre, Centenary Square provides an extensive brick-paved space for exhibitions and events – open-air concerts and arts festivals. This is the classic role of a big central public-events square, so common in mainland European cities but rare in Britain and new to Birmingham. The richness of its multi-coloured brick paving, carefully detailed stonework and solid cast-iron street furniture, plus its central fountain, combine to achieve a comfortable and welcoming public realm. The artists Tess Jaray and Tom Lomax collaborated with the City Council's architects on the design and detailing. The *Forward* statue by Raymond Mason still generates controversy. If it had been metal rather than glass fibre it might have been accepted more easily in this metal-bashing city. In the evenings when the bars and clubs of Broad Street and Brindleyplace are in full swing, Centenary Square is a place to meet and to promenade.

THE MIDLANDS

LOCATION accessed from Broad Street to the south; via the International Convention Centre to the west and the Central Library to the east
LOCAL AUTHORITY Birmingham City Council

Birmingham City Council, Department of Planning and Architecture

BIRMINGHAM: BRINDLEYPLACE SQUARE

In 1995, an extraordinary sight appeared in Birmingham. For years, the cleared site which was to become the Brindleyplace development remained void as developers merged, departed or went bust. Then behind the completed first phase of development (the canal-side bars and restaurants called The Water's Edge), the surface of a new square was placed in the desert. Fountains played, water ran across immaculate curving stone steps, young maple and gingko trees sprang into leaf. On three sides the new square was surrounded by empty dereliction – a surreal scene, but commercially shrewd.

The square is now enclosed by five new buildings, two designed by Allies and Morrison, others by Demetri Porphyrios, Sidell Gibson, and Stanton Williams. The Porphyrios building has the commanding position, and whether or not one likes its classical pretensions, addresses the square very strongly. Like the others, its ground floor is arcaded as required by the masterplan. A glass café designed by Piers Gough (CZWG Architects) sits diagonally in the centre of the square. This contradicts Camillo Sitte's advice that the centre of squares be left empty, but the Bar Rouge is so small and decorative that it is really an ornament rather than an obstruction.

Six years on, Brindleyplace Square is on everyone's mental map and is well used. The space is theatrical, and the behaviour of people in it, strolling up and down and looking around, tends to be rather selfconscious. One suspects that many of us are half-imagining we are in Italy, taking our *passeggiata* along the city's chain of new or redesigned squares. Sitting with a café au lait outside the Bar Rouge, one is conscious that we are playing a role – the English as new Europeans, at home in our public urban living rooms.

LOCATION to the north and west of Symphony Hall and International Convention Centre
LOCAL AUTHORITY Birmingham City Council

masterplan John Chatwin in succession to Terry Farrell Partnership

BIRMINGHAM: GAS STREET BASIN

Both the Convention Centre and Brindleyplace developments make the most of their canalside setting, with restaurants, bars, bridges and sitting areas focusing on the canal with its frequent boat traffic. The canals themselves have been dramatically enhanced in recent year with clean water, brick-paved towpaths and restored listed buildings encouraging exploration of the 'secret world' of the maze of narrow waterways that focus on Gas Street Basin. The grime of the industrial past has gone and some of the building details are dubious 'modern heritage' but the overall effect is a vibrant and welcoming place at the heart of the activities of the Broad Street area. Enough of the old has been kept to connect visitors with the history of the canals which kick-started Birmingham's rapid industrial expansion in the 19th century. The canals do not just attract visitors – the network of towpaths has become busy with joggers escaping office routine and, at Brindleyplace and Gas Street, canalside housing has brought residents into the heart of Birmingham. The towpath connects through to the Mailbox, the converted central sorting office, as part of a route back to New Street station. The Mailbox is an ingenious conversion into a mixed-use development containing shopping, restaurants and bars topped off with new roof-level apartments. Even the BBC has been attracted to relocate here, away from Pebble Mill.

THE MIDLANDS

LOCATION Gas Street Basin can be accessed by canal, from the west from Brindleyplace Square, from Broad Street to the south
LOCAL AUTHORITY Birmingham City Council

British Waterways Authority

CHESTERFIELD: MARKET SQUARE

Chesterfield's market square was threatened with comprehensive development in the early 1970s. This was successfully resisted and the open square was retained and improved, together with an enlarged market hall and major development on the south side. The new development utilises existing properties on Low Pavement as part of additional shopping provision and this is linked to carparks across Beetwell Street. The Market Hall, originally built in 1857, has been refurbished and extended, the Market Place improved and a new shopping mall integrated with restored properties from different periods. Taken together, these elements have contributed to the revitalisation of the town centre while retaining the best from the past and ensuring that the characteristic market square remains an integral part of Chesterfield's shopping experience. Don't forget to stroll along to see the leaning spire of St Mary's church.

LOCATION parking accessible from Beetwell Street in the town centre
LOCAL AUTHORITY Chesterfield District Council

Feilden & Mawson, Elsom Pack & Roberts Partnership

HEREFORD: LEFT BANK VILLAGE

Adjacent to the river and the old Wye Bridge is an exciting development known as the Left Bank Village. It consists of a new building with riverside terraces, the reuse of existing buildings by the riverside and street-frontage properties which have additions to the rear that reflect the animation of the new building. On the riverside there is also an open paved area, known as Kate's Square, where open-air entertainments are held (flamenco evenings, jazz, country and western and other musical entertainment). An adjacent warehouse building is available for larger gatherings. The three-storeyed new building contains bars, restaurants and meeting space, La Rive restaurant, the River Terrace and the Charles Bar with attractive views over the river and to the cathedral. Gwynne Street, which is the service access to the development, has been delightfully designed as the front door to parts of the development, faced by the colourful rear extensions to occupiers such as a delicatessen and patisserie. It also provides access to some of the remaining warehouses that were served from the river.

Gwynne Street connects to Broad Street which gives access to the cathedral area where the *Mappa Mundi* is housed in a recent building by William Whitfield. Hereford has an extensive pedestrian area. Another building of interest is All Saints church in the main shopping street, imaginatively altered to include a café.

THE MIDLANDS

LOCATION on the riverside next to the old Wye Bridge, accessible from Bridge Street
LOCAL AUTHORITY Hereford City Council

Angus Jamieson Architect and Richard Hemingway Architects

LEICESTER: BEDE ISLAND NORTH

Former derelict railway land to the west of the the city centre has been redeveloped to provide a mixture of uses, at the centre of which is a public space, four shops and a public house and restaurant. The overall scheme is a thriving example of inner-city regeneration with a range of housing, a successful business park and open space serving the wider area. City Challenge funding provided the basis for the project. There are close connections to the De Montford campus across the river Soar and the area relates to a main cycleway running throughout the city. The Quay public house is a converted pumping station which overlooks a hard-paved square within which seating and public art are arranged. A new 2-hectare park adjacent to this acts as the break between the business-park and residential uses (housing association, privately rented and student accommodation). The main pedestrian link through the park and the square provide direct routes from the university and city centre to adjacent housing areas.

Leicester has an extensive pedestrianised city centre, and the Humberstone Gate area is worth a visit. In that case interesting paving patterns related to adjacent buildings and simple street furniture enhance the accessible shopping area.

THE MIDLANDS

LOCATION 800 metres west of city centre, immediately west of De Montford University
LOCAL AUTHORITY Leicester City Council

Urban Design Group, Leicester City Council

NOTTINGHAM: CASTLE WHARF

'A good city is like a good party … people stay for hours' (Jan Gehl). It follows that a good place is like a good party … and, in turn, people will stay and use the place for hours. Castle Wharf has been hailed as a commercial success, spearheading a rejuvenated interest in Nottingham's 'southside' regarded as pleasing by some and less so by others. Castle Wharf is attractively designed, fitting well into its location, relating well to the waterside and a comfortable place to socialise in the evenings. The heart of the Wharf is centred around the British Waterways building, two new bar-and-eateries and a comedy club. The area has soared in popularity with 20-somethings who frequent the bars in the evenings spilling out on to the terraces during the warmer months. In contrast, the area is largely devoid of activity in the daytime with the exception of local office workers. Many would find it hard to fault the development and a lot of people enjoy spending time with friends here. However, such places can perhaps be criticised for being socially restrictive with evening activity anchored on young drinkers. There are no other uses to attract or cater for other sections of society – is this the way to design good places?

Elsewhere in Nottingham the Inland Revenue Headquarters, to the west of Castle Wharf along the canal, and the Castlegate Costume and Textile Museum, just to the north in Castle Road, are worth visiting.

LOCATION Castle Wharf is almost immediately north of Nottingham Midland station over the Carrington Street Bridge
LOCAL AUTHORITY Nottingham City Council

John Dixon Associates and Franklin Ellis Architects

NOTTINGHAM: PLAYHOUSE SQUARE

Changes made since the original theatre was designed have created a vibrant place animated by the spectacular *Sky Mirror*. When Peter Moro's Playhouse design was originally built there was a road in front providing parking, which formed part of Wellington Circus. One arm of the Circus was subsequently closed to provide a space related to the Playhouse but the full benefit was not felt until the space was redesigned. A first floor added above the Limelight bar in 1994 provided new rehearsal space and more enclosure on the eastern edge. The major redesign of the square began later and included the installation of the *Sky Mirror* by Anish Kapoor, completed in 2001. The *Sky Mirror* is a polished steel mirror 6 metres in diameter, tipped back at its vertical axis by 16 degrees to reflect the sky and surrounding buildings and facing 7 degrees east of north to avoid eye-damaging reflections. It is mounted on a plinth-cum-water feature which accommodates the slope in the site at this point. The lower part of the square relates to the lower Playhouse bar where the reverse side of the mirror and its different reflections are experienced. The square is finished in contrasting granite paving and specially designed seats and a new glazed canopy to the Limelight bar complement the space. It is known as the Djanogly Playground and it should also be visited in the dark to appreciate the subtlety of the lighting scheme which adds sparkle to an exciting place.

LOCATION North Cross Street on the north-west side of the city centre, accessible off Derby Road, adjacent to the Albert Hall
LOCAL AUTHORITY Nottingham City Council

Marsh and Grochowski Architects and Anish Kapoor

NORTH-WEST ENGLAND AND NORTH WALES

INTRODUCTION 7.2

BOLTON: VICTORIA SQUARE 7.4

CHESTER: CITY CENTRE 7.6

LIVERPOOL: ALBERT DOCK 7.8

LIVERPOOL: CONCERT SQUARE 7.10

LIVERPOOL: DERBY SQUARE 7.12

LIVERPOOL: PIER HEAD 7.14

MANCHESTER: ALBERT SQUARE 7.16

MANCHESTER: CASTLEFIELD 7.18

MANCHESTER: EXCHANGE SQUARE 7.20

MANCHESTER: GREAT NORTHERN SQUARE 7.22

PORTMEIRION 7.24

PRESTON: MARKET SQUARE 7.26

RUNCORN: HALTON BROW 7.28

SALFORD: THE LOWRY PLAZA 7.30

WHITEHAVEN: WATERFRONT 7.32

WIGAN: MARKET PLACE 7.34

INTRODUCTION

This region contains the metropolitan areas of Manchester and Liverpool, to the south of these Chester and Crewe, and to the north Preston, Lancaster, the Lake District and Carlisle. The coastal edge runs from the Dee and Mersey estuaries up to the Ribble and Morecambe Bay, ending at the Solway Firth. North Wales has also been grouped with the north-west as access naturally links the two areas along the Welsh coast at least as far as Caernarvon.

The region provides many examples of the urban changes brought on by the industrial revolution – none better than the rapid growth of Greater Manchester where a number of 19th-century cotton mills remain, some converted to community or residential use. In public-space terms, fragments of the medieval layout can still be seen in St Ann's Square, now largely closed to traffic, and the early Moravian community of Fairfield of 1783 remains in the east of the city. The major civic space of Albert Square, with Waterhouse's competition-winning town hall, reflects the vigour of the Victorian period when much of the central area was constructed. Most recently the Urban Development Corporation invested considerably in areas such as Castlefield. The IRA bomb in 1996 led to opportunities for replanning some of the post-war development in the vicinity of the cathedral.

Liverpool's former maritime importance resulted in major buildings on the Mersey waterfront. Important examples include the now-converted Albert Dock and the pierhead group of the Liver, the Mersey Docks and Harbour Board and Cunard buildings. The elegant town hall dating from 1754 is laid out on an axis with Castle Street and the Queen Anne buildings of the Bluecoat Chambers provide an attractive outdoor space and arts centre close to the main shopping centre. Next to Lime Street station stands the impressive Victorian civic group of St George's Hall and the City Museums and Art Galleries, complemented by St John's Gardens. The city's two cathedrals are located on higher ground at opposite ends of Hope Street, the Anglican cathedral providing adjacent spaces of particular character.

On the southern side of the Mersey, Birkenhead has an attractive civic space in Hamilton Square, due to be improved, and it includes the earliest public park, designed by Joseph Paxton. Port Sunlight, a community developed by the Lever family, is an enlightened vision of industrial patronage. The post-war new towns of Runcorn and Warrington (both in fact expanded towns) lie to the south and the north of the Mersey respectively. Skelmersdale New Town lies further inland to the north and the Leyland/Chorley area was also selected as an area for additional planned growth.

Chester, first settled by the Romans, is distinguished by its medieval rows now used as two-level shopping. The Roman town forms the basis for today's central street pattern which is given added definition by the remaining city walls. Its attractive river frontage is overlooked by Thomas Harrison's rebuilt castle and county buildings.

Further north, Preston and Lancaster provide the locations for county administration. The historic city of Lancaster is identified from the motorway by the domed Ashton Memorial and was chosen as one of the sites for a new university in the 1960s. Further north, Kendal is the largest town in the Lake District and is noted for its yards, narrow streets located at right angles to the main streets. Cartmel and Kirkby Lonsdale, the latter a charming market town, are well worth a visit.

North Wales contains a large number of seaside resorts such as Rhyl and Llandudno; towns with an important historic heritage include Conwy, Beaumaris and Caernarvon. Portmeirion, featured as a 'good place', lies on the coast of Cardigan Bay just to the north of Harlech Castle and south-west of Snowdonia.

BOLTON: VICTORIA SQUARE

Victoria Square and the town hall form the civic and physical heart of Bolton. The square is the major node of the pedestrianisation network and the reference point for the visual interpretation of the town. The refurbishment of the square was completed in August 1999. The design aimed to create a public space in which people could take pride and where they would feel comfortable. It was important to create a dignified setting while simultaneously retaining a space in which events could be held. The square's design uses high-quality materials. Moving away from modern man-made materials and using bold, simple styles, Victoria Square aimed to be at the forefront of urban design. The natural stone flags complement the town hall and add warmth to the square while stainless steel and polished granite impart style. Specially designed street furniture incorporates a town guide and street maps for both the visually impaired and the blind.

Bolton's museum displays Samuel Crompton's 'spinning mule'.

LOCATION in the centre of the town and easily accessed from Bolton station via Newport Street. While the square is pedestrianised, parking is conveniently located and accessible from the M61

LOCAL AUTHORITY Bolton Metropolitan Borough Council

Bolton Metropolitan Borough Council

CHESTER: CITY CENTRE

The centre of Chester is of immense historical significance – near the cathedral, within the ancient circuit of the city walls and at the heart of Chester's system of medieval 'rows'. Yet this area around Bridge Street and Eastgate Street is also an enjoyable contemporary pedestrian shopping area. It is a perfect example of how conservation can work in tandem with economic development. The evocative environment of the historic cityscape increases the commercial viability of the town centre and, in turn, this commercial success provides the necessary capital for continuing urban conservation.

The Rows are a system of 13th-century walkways on the first floor of the major streets in the centre of Chester. They make it possible to shop on two levels. In fact, many of the medieval timber-framed buildings in these streets are Victorian reinterpretations of the local vernacular black-and-white style. Despite their age, The Rows still work as retail premises, housing cafés, shoe-repair shops, bookstores and small offices. The double level of The Rows allows high-turnover chainstores to exist directly below unique local shops.

Chester's city walls are almost complete and provide a good perambulation from which to view the city.

LOCATION Chester's station is remote from the town centre, down City Road and west along Foregate Street. There are good carparks
LOCAL AUTHORITY Chester City Council

Chester City Council

LIVERPOOL: ALBERT DOCK

Now converted into a modern multi-use complex containing the Liverpool Maritime Museum, the Tate Liverpool gallery, the Beatles' Story, Granada TV studios, apartments, offices, and shops, Albert Dock has become a vibrant pedestrian space too. Designed in 1839 by Jesse Hartley, it opened in 1846. It was designed to be secure and fireproof employing iron and brick construction and enclosing the central pool with warehouses. The functional architecture of the docks has it own beauty that still impresses. The five-storey warehouses that surround the dock are supported on the ground floor by massive Doric cast-iron columns. Other details of the dock's innovative construction can be seen in the iron cross-braces on the upper floors and in the flat-arched brick floor supports. The dock was closed in 1972 and nearly demolished but by 1984 it was completely restored. The pool within the dock is often busy during the summer. Now, throughout the year residents and visitors stroll underneath the long covered ground-floor walkways. The Albert Dock is a truly successful example of the adaptation of historic buildings for modern use.

Liverpool's two 20th-century cathedrals and the new Watersports Centre in the Queen's Dock (Marks Barfield Architects) are worth visiting.

LOCATION about 2.5 kilometres west of Liverpool Lime Street station, on the waterfront
LOCAL AUTHORITY Liverpool City Council

Franklin Stafford Partnership

LIVERPOOL: CONCERT SQUARE

The Concert Square scheme created a lively new public square adjacent to a high-quality mixed-use development. A previously derelict and hostile backwater has been transformed by selective demolition, refurbishment and new build, reinventing the urban context of the site. The public square has become a focal point for the area and the scheme includes apartments, a café, bars and restaurants, studio offices and a gallery.

The main Concert Square buildings were acquired by developers/designers Urban Splash in 1994 when what had been a chemical factory became vacant. The design team was asked to propose a comprehensive urban-design solution which realised the potential of the area by creating a public space and an environment suitable for uses including Liverpool's first loft apartments. The scheme has been described as 'a collaboration between a developer and the local authority… and is about making outside spaces; it is about modernity, consistency and solidity of detailing, it is about the integration of graphic design, landscape and architecture in a speculative market… it is above all providing good value for money, and above all it is about regeneration.'

LOCATION between Wood Street and Fleet Street, south-west of Bold Street and northeast of Duke Street, on the eastern edge of the city centre
LOCAL AUTHORITY Liverpool City Council

Urban Splash

LIVERPOOL: DERBY SQUARE

Derby Square formed part of the site of St George's church. It was used by John Foster as the centre of an imaginative plan to create a circus at a cross axis between the newly widened Lord Street and Castle Street which extended south to the monumental Customs House. The Customs House, Lord Street, St George's Crescent and South Castle Street were destroyed in World War II, the church having been demolished in 1897; the post-war replacements are a poor substitute for this grand conception. Castle Street is a major street in the city centre culminating at one end in the delicately scaled town hall (John Wood, James Wyatt and John Foster, 1749–1807) and at the other end in Derby Square, within which is located the large-scale Victoria Monument. This forms a major element in the open space defined by the high law courts building and on the east and west sides by office buildings with commercial or army-recruitment uses at ground level. The space would be immeasurably improved if more gregarious uses occupied the ground-floor spaces and the paving outside – despite the often windy micro-climate. The monument, completed in 1906, is somewhat overscaled and some even consider it to be obscene although it is generally recognised as an 'epitome of Victorian self confidence'. Manchester has its Albert Memorial, Liverpool the Victoria Monument.

LOCATION southern end of Castle Street
LOCAL AUTHORITY Liverpool City Council

City Coordinating Group, Liverpool City Council

LIVERPOOL: THE PIER HEAD

The Pier Head is a symbol of Liverpool's maritime history: ferries still cross the river Mersey from here. Liverpool's zenith was reached at the beginning of the 20th century with the construction of the iconic 'Three Graces': the Royal Liver Friendly Society, the Mersey Docks and Harbour Board and the Cunard office buildings, in spirit profoundly expressive of the imperial optimism of Edwardian enterprise. It is these three buildings that form the spectacular backdrop to the Pier Head urban space. The growth of the docks on which Liverpool's wealth and trade were based was accompanied by the development of commercial premises in the older city centre. The Pier Head was constructed on land gained by filling in the Georges Dock. It gave Liverpool its world-famous skyline, reminiscent of the great North American cities with which its principal trade was then carried out.

For a long time the Pier Head was used as the city's bus depot but the buses were removed in 1992 and a 3-hectare public space was laid out with lawns, walkways and a bandstand, providing a proper setting for the equestrian statue of Edward VII. An unattractive café building remains.

LOCATION on the waterfront to the north of Albert Dock and at the foot of Dale Street
LOCAL AUTHORITY Liverpool City Council

Allies and Morrison Architects

MANCHESTER: ALBERT SQUARE

Albert Square is Manchester's principal civic space and demonstrates the value of simple but robust design principles in accommodating a diverse range of public events and activities. The layout of the square in its present form is about 15 years old although the basic form was determined more than a century ago when Alfred Waterhouse won the competition for the town hall. The Albert Memorial, designed by Thomas Worthington, had already been built in front of the site. For most of the 20th century roads dominated the square, leaving only a meagre central island for pedestrians. Major public events such as rallies and receptions for sporting champions have traditionally taken place in Albert Square but involved road closures and crowd-control measures. The design solution to this was the closure of the section of road outside the town hall, which was accompanied by complete repaving, replacement of underground toilets by new accessible facilities in the town hall extension, a new lighting system and a small number of very carefully located trees. Granite setts were used for the central portion of the square to meet the intense pressures of usage expected in the central performance part of the space. This was laid to falls without steps for safety and flexibility of use. York stone flags are used for the perimeter, helping all users to gain easy access.

LOCATION north-west of the town hall adjoining Princess Street. Closest Metro stop is St Peter's Square

LOCAL AUTHORITY Manchester City Council

Manchester City Council City Architects Department

MANCHESTER: CASTLEFIELD

The wider Castlefield area demonstrates the selective restoration and redevelopment of an area of exceptional heritage value. The heritage status is worthy of special mention because of its remarkable layering of land uses and urban form over time. Whereas many other heritage sites are notable for a specific period of history or a particular type of land use, Castlefield has been the scene of successive waves of occupation, including a Roman fort, river and canal navigation and warehousing, the world's first passenger railway station (on Liverpool Road), and various 20th-century interventions. The formal designation of the area as an Urban Heritage Park has helped in providing focus and has paid dividends. Castlefield is marketed as an educational facility, leisure destination and for commercial and residential regeneration re-using the canal warehouses and railway arches in new ways. The city council led the initial planning vision which was supported by Greater Manchester County Council. Substantial investment came from the Central Manchester Development Corporation which also established a management company.

For those wishing to walk across the city centre, the Rochdale Canal provides an interesting cross-section running from Dukes 92 pub, behind G-Mex (the former Central station), alongside Canal Street, the lively centre of the gay community, to the basin beyond Piccadilly Station. The canal then continues into Ancoats, the site of the first urban steam mills and the next area for regeneration.

LOCATION west of Deansgate and south of Liverpool Road. Metro stop G-Mex
LOCAL AUTHORITY Manchester City Council

design coordination Central Manchester Development Corporation

MANCHESTER: EXCHANGE SQUARE

The 1996 IRA bomb in Manchester city centre provided an opportunity to replan the area between the cathedral and St Ann's Square and establish a continuation of urban form that did not exist in the previous redevelopment. EDAW's masterplan included a new triangular space between the old Corn Exchange and the new Marks & Spencer development. The detailed layout uses parallel ramps defined by walls which also serve as seating. A long water feature runs through the space following the line of Hanging Ditch, a famous medieval Manchester landmark. A series of angled windmills (designed by artist John Hyatt) is placed in front of the M&S building.

One critic commented that the design was 'insensitive to context and shows signs of lack of understanding between designers and realisers in much of the detail. On the other hand, a landscape architect with a track record of original and provocative schemes has brought a refreshingly playful and dynamic approach to a Mancunian public space'. A new pedestrian street links the square through to St Ann's Square, an area formerly congested by traffic seeking somewhere to park. This specialist shopping area, together with the adjacent King Street, connected through St Ann's Passage, provides a civilised shopping environment with well-considered hard landscape. See also Barton Arcade on the northern side of St Ann's Square.

LOCATION south of Victoria station and Manchester cathedral adjacent to Corporation Street. Metro stop Victoria Station
LOCAL AUTHORITY Manchester City Council

landscape architect Martha Schwartz

MANCHESTER: GREAT NORTHERN SQUARE

This is an imaginative new square in an area of the city where theatres, the convention centre and the main concert hall are located. It gets its name from the retained Great Northern Railway Warehouse, listed grade II, which forms one side to the new space.

The existing warehouse has been converted to provide bars, restaurants and clubs at the Deansgate level. A plaza level above this provides access to a large number of shops, a glazed atrium and a 16-screen multiplex cinema. Above the plaza level the existing building accommodates parking. The new public square includes an amphitheatre looking towards the triangular pavilion – Bar 38 – which provides space on three levels. New cafés and bars in the warehouse also front on to this space. Tree planting and a water feature complement the amphitheatre geometry.

The adjacent site to the east includes the G-Mex exhibition centre which was formerly Central station, one of three rail termini in the city centre. Next to this is the new concert hall, the Bridgewater Hall (designed by RHWL), which was part-funded by the adjacent office development. The space between the different uses, Barbirolli Square, is flanked by new offices and the concert hall and encompasses a branch of the canal system which links into the Rochdale Canal both as a waterway and a pedestrian route. Steps and ramps down to the canal also lead to a bar and restaurant.

LOCATION at the junction of Peter Street and Deansgate on the south-west side of the city centre
LOCAL AUTHORITY Manchester City Council

Skidmore Owings and Merrill with Leslie Jones Architects

PORTMEIRION

The creation of an Italian village over 50 years (1925–75) on the shores of a damp estuary in north Wales seems an unlikely occurrence. Portmeirion shows, however, that imagination can triumph over reality. But to be successful that imagination must be strong and wise. The creator of Portmeirion, Clough Williams-Ellis (1883–1984), was a strong-willed and forceful visionary. When considered against rational criteria Portmeirion is difficult to justify as a 'good place'. It is new building in an area of outstanding natural beauty; it is exclusive and entry is both restricted and must be paid for. Yet once within the 'village', the spirit soars; architecture and artefacts delight the eye. New and reconstructed buildings complement the landform, trees and planting complement the buildings. Far from damaging the sublime setting, the assembly enhances the scene. The village also includes a pottery and a good hotel.

A unique vision in the outstanding setting of the Snowdonia National Park, Portmeirion is well worth a journey through some of Britain's finest scenery.

LOCATION access is simplest by car and the A387. But you can travel by train to Porthmadog (Portmadoc) and from there by bus to Portmeirion
LOCAL AUTHORITY Gwynedd County Council

Clough Williams-Ellis

PRESTON: MARKET SQUARE

Preston has a long history, but it is now essentially a Victorian town, a strategically placed junction of several transport systems. The north-west's third city, it has had the 'new town' treatment, and is now well looked after. But that is only the beginning. The Market Square has for centuries been Preston's central space. Dramatic enclosing buildings combine with upgraded paving and street furniture in adjacent spaces using bollards, seats and lamps to make it an enjoyable and largely pedestrian area. The ancient market cross survives, and there is a fine war memorial.

The Harris Museum and Art Gallery dominates the square to the east; this is a splendid late-classical building (look inside, too). On the north side is the equally sophisticated County Sessions House. Closing this vista, down Harris Street, is the Guildhall. The south side is a sad pile of 1960s offices on the site of the burned-down gothic-revival town hall. To the west remains a hint of the smaller-scale buildings. To the north is the large main post office, no more than an acceptable enclosing block. The battle of the styles raged here, but since the buildings are of similar stone, mellowed with age, it seems now all of a piece.

The Preston Docks regeneration by the river Ribble, with a new locomotive shed, is nearby.

LOCATION Market Square is 1.5 kilometres east of Preston station up Fishergate and Birley Street. The bus station is just off the square
LOCAL AUTHORITY Preston Borough Council

Preston Borough Council

RUNCORN: HALTON BROW

Set in one of Britain's second generation of new towns, the Halton Brow neighbourhood marks a radical change in the layout of public housing – a reaction against both the industrialised high-rise systems popular in the mid 1960s and the Radburn pattern, with its separation of cars and pedestrians. When completed in 1967 it represented a pioneering attempt to subordinate the car. This is a place in which children can play and where elderly people can move around in safety. Here footpaths are more important than roads and garage courts are replaced by 'parking squares'. These squares are heavily mounded and planted to provide a green outlook from the surrounding houses, but casual supervision is still possible. The layout is a grid of footpaths and roadways. Sightlines and road widths are deliberately restricted and radii kept tight to reduce traffic speed. After a decade of use the only recorded accident involved a drunken pedestrian colliding with a stationary car! Emergency services reported that access for ambulances and fire engines through the site was easier than in traditional housing areas.

The houses, built in a 'rationalised traditional' style, may appear gloomy on a dull day. Using mellow brown brick and concrete roof tiles, the development reflects the sandstone used in the original Halton village. Generously planted, the scheme has matured well. The local centre, pub and sheltered housing have survived less well.

LOCATION take the busway from Runcorn station to Halton village. By car, take Central Expressway to its junction with Halton Road
LOCAL AUTHORITY Halton Borough Council

Runcorn Development Corporation

SALFORD: THE LOWRY PLAZA

The Lowry in the Salford Quays development provides cultural facilities in a stunning land-mark building by Michael Wilford & Associates. It has gathered around it a designer-outlet shopping centre; across the Ship Canal is the Imperial War Museum North designed by Daniel Libeskind. A paved plaza between the Lowry and the shopping centre provides an outdoor performance area capable of holding up to 8000 people. The infrastructure which was installed before development is of a high standard, with the detailing of the quays, natural paving, tree planting and street furniture providing a robust framework within which individual developments are located. This work was coordinated by Shepheard, Epstein and Hunter. The Metrolink service connects the area to central Manchester. Not all development is of the quality of the Lowry area which is given an added identity by a 14-storey block of flats with a distinct marine flavour. A spectacular lifting bridge links the Lowry area across the Manchester Ship Canal to the Imperial War Museum.

The Lowry is an intricate building on many levels. It includes the 1700-seat Lyric Theatre and the 480-seat Quays Theatre, a permanent Lowry gallery and other exhibition space. These are complemented by children's artwork areas, cafés and restaurants. Its exterior uses curved elements and a circular tower clad in stainless steel – particularly dramatic at night due to a spectacular lighting scheme. The shopping centre, designed by RTKL, contains about 60 shopping units, cinemas, a food court and various restaurants.

The whole development makes a major statement and gives substance to the claims that the conurbation has a new gateway.

LOCATION Salford Quays, 2.4 kilometres west of Manchester city centre; also accessible from Metrolink, Harbour City stop
LOCAL AUTHORITY Salford City Council

RTKL Architects

WHITEHAVEN: WATERFRONT

Whitehaven's totally revitalised waterfront provides an attractive setting for events and complements the traditional town centre. The town, developed in the 17th and 18th centuries by the Lowther family, was reputedly designed by Christopher Wren. It has a gridiron plan with public buildings, vistas and open spaces as important components. Less than 200 years ago the port was second only to London but the decline of traditional industries and the tidal nature of the harbour led to steady decline.

The borough council recognised that action needed to be taken and an urban regeneration company was established, a harbour strategy prepared and financial support obtained from various bodies including European funds and Lottery money. The result is a lock-controlled harbour which is not only used as a marina but also as an important commercial fishing centre. A new museum, The Beacon, tells the story of Whitehaven's social, maritime and industrial history and the Rum Story is located nearby on Lowther Street.

Much of the quayside is restricted to pedestrians and public art with maritime themes enlivens the quaysides, where the detailed design was carried out by Building Design Partnership. Along the quay known as Lime Tongue a wave structure runs towards a vertical crow's-nest feature set on an axis with the town's layout. A tented structure on East Strand provides space for weekend markets and events such as the Maritime Festival draw thousands of visitors to the town. An important aspect of the development has been the establishment of a management organisation, with funds, to continue the work initiated by the regeneration company.

LOCATION on the harbourside at the end of Lowther and Duke Streets
LOCAL AUTHORITY Copeland Borough Council

masterplans Llewelyn-Davies and Jon Rowland Urban Design

WIGAN: MARKET PLACE

The Market Place and parish church form the core of historic Wigan. In the past this was the focus of a daily market and the site of regular fairs. The opening of the Market Hall in the 19th century and the Galleries Shopping Centre in the late 1970s removed the Market Place's commercial role. In spite of partial pedestrianisation, the fine buildings around the square were becoming under-used. An urban-design strategy was prepared that sought not only to create a high-quality space but would also encourage increased use and investment in the area to restore its status as the civic heart of the town.

The key element in the new square is a slightly elevated platform which creates a sheltered pedestrian area where people can relax on benches in the sun. A large mosaic forms the centrepiece and commemorates Wigan's 13th-century royal charter. The carriageway has been narrowed to ensure that pedestrians can enjoy free movement. Already the usage of surrounding buildings is improving but there is some way to go before Market Place becomes the vibrant area it must once have been.

Wigan Pier, made famous by George Orwell, is to be found on the banks of the Leeds and Liverpool Canal as it passes through Wigan. Canalside buildings have been converted to new uses and a museum, pub and restaurant attract many visitors to this landmark site.

LOCATION to the north of Wigan's North Western and Wallgate stations, up Wallgate
LOCAL AUTHORITY Wigan Borough Council

Wigan Borough Council

NORTHERN ENGLAND

INTRODUCTION 8.2
BRIDLINGTON: SOUTH PROMENADE 8.4
DURHAM: CITY CENTRE 8.6
HULL: MARKET SQUARE 8.8
LEEDS: MILLENNIUM SQUARE 8.10
LEEDS: THE CALLS 8.12
LEEDS: VICTORIA QUARTER 8.14
NEWCASTLE UPON TYNE: BYKER 8.16
NEWCASTLE UPON TYNE: EAST QUAYSIDE 8.18
NEWCASTLE UPON TYNE: GRAINGER TOWN 8.20
SHEFFIELD: PEACE GARDENS 8.22
SHEFFIELD: VICTORIA QUAYS 8.24
SUNDERLAND: ST PETER'S RIVERSIDE 8.26
WAKEFIELD: KIRKGATE 8.28
YORK RIVERSIDE 8.30
YORK: ST MARY'S SQUARE 8.32

INTRODUCTION

The northern region in this book comprises Yorkshire, Durham and Northumberland.

Sheffield and Rotherham in South Yorkshire were centres of the steel industry and have now diversified into the service sector so that infrastructure such as canals are used for leisure purposes (page 8.24), while a former steel mill has been converted (by WIlkinson Eyre) into the Magna Centre, with a spectacular educational theme.

The metropolitan area of West Yorkshire includes Leeds, Bradford, Huddersfield and Halifax. Here the woollen industry traditionally provided employment. Now many of the previously numerous woollen mills have disappeared or have been converted to new uses such as small business centres and craft locations, as in Halifax or Little Germany in Bradford. Piece Hall in Halifax, completed in 1779 for traders to display their cloths, remains as a symbol of that age. The community of Saltaire, built in 1851, was the industrialist Titus Salt's reaction to what was often desparate urban squalor. The mill now houses a gallery and businesses. Victorian commercial vigour is expressed in Leeds in the civic buildings located on The Headrow, the town hall being designed by Cuthbert Broderick. Leeds has continued to develop as the major commercial centre of the area. Harrogate – with its spa and the attractive open space of The Stray – provided one of the residential areas serving the city. The cathedral town of Ripon, the monasteries such as Fountains Abbey and the Minsters at Beverley and York reflect the religious foundations of the medieval period.

York is a fine city where medieval streets and much of the city walls still remain. One of the latest additions to the area, York University at Heslington, was created in the 1960s to meet the growth in demand for higher education. Hull (more formally Kingston upon Hull) retains part of its historic past in the Market Square (8.8). A number of the older docks have been filled in, some to provide open space while new housing clusters around docks now used as marinas. On the coast north of Hull there are a number of holiday resorts, including Scarborough and Bridlington (page 8.4) where an imaginative new promenade and facilities, including public art, have been installed.

The national parks in the North York Moors and the Yorkshire Dales contain many attractive villages (Coxwold, Grassington and Dent). On the eastern edge of the Dales, the incomparable market town of Richmond has a sloping and cobbled marketplace overlooked by a Norman castle.

Durham's majestic cathedral stands high up within the oxbow of the river Wear. Close-by are the castle and the older colleges of the university on North and South Bailey, a delightful area to wander through (page 8.6). Gateshead, with a progressive public-art policy commissioned Anthony Gormley's monumental *Angel of the North* to act as a landmark, seen both from the road and rail lines. Alongside the river Tyne, Gateshead has commissioned the new Baltic Centre for Contemporary Art and the forthcoming Music Centre. The two banks of the river are already connected by the spectacular 'winking eye' pedestrian bridge, Gateshead's Millennium project. The Newcastle side has already been redeveloped to take advantage of its setting (page 8.18). Newcastle's neoclassical centre, created by Grainger and Dobson, is being revitalised (page 8.20) to counter out of town competitors such as the Metro Centre.

Declining employment in mining and other traditional industries led to the designation of new towns in Newton Aycliffe and Peterlee in the 1940s and in Washington in the 1960s. The artist Victor Pasmore was involved in the design of new housing areas in Peterlee. Outside the main communities the villages of Staindrop and Blanchland and Alston, Hexham, Alnwick, Warkworth and Lindisfarne all repay a visit and the border town of Berwick on Tweed provides the ramparts and fortifications appropriate to its location.

BRIDLINGTON: SOUTH PROMENADE

An outstanding example of the innovative improvement of a traditional resort, building in humour and fun. The remodelled South Promenade stretches along about half of the town's seafront and is a combination of modern design and public art with a running text by Mel Gooding and various works by Bruce McLean. The town's history is traced in text along the paved promenade with cafés and changing facilities adding a magical touch to a visit to the seaside. These elements run along one nautical mile, stretching south from the harbour which is a base for a small fishing fleet and leisure craft. Along the front of the promenade is Mel Gooding's whimsical poem, set in terrazzo, and behind that a long narrow pool creates a moat in front of the new beach huts. Larger buildings are set below the cliff providing a series of terraces leading to the beach. The existing sea wall runs along the sand from the harbour to McLean's coloured jetty marking the end of the urban beach and terminating in the Headland Café.

NORTHERN ENGLAND

LOCATION south of Bridlington Harbour
LOCAL AUTHORITY East Riding Borough Council,
succeeded by East Riding of Yorkshire Council

Bauman Lyons Architects and Bruce McLean

DURHAM: CITY CENTRE

Durham's Centre changed over five years from a dangerous, highly congested and
environmentally decadent area to one where, on the peninsula and its bridges and the new
shopping centre, it is a delight to walk, shop and admire a townscape of distinction.

A new road scheme which bypassed the historic centre of the city was completed in 1975 and provided the opportunity to remove vehicular traffic together with signs, traffic lights and bus shelters. The floorscaping scheme set out to establish a high quality of design using traditional materials imaginatively employed. The scheme involved the repaving of 10,000 square metres of streets and spaces at the core of the 'outstanding conservation area' – part of North Road, Framwellgate Bridge, Silver Street leading up the hill to the Market Place and Elvet Street – and was completed in 1978. Three materials were used: York stone paving flags for predominantly pedestrian areas, York stone setts for pedestrian streets and the Market Place service area, and asphalt with a York stone chipping finish for traffic streets. A distinctive detail is the use of parallel tracks or wheelers within the setted area to define routes for service vehicles – a detail that is found in many historic streets, but often excluded today as being impractical. The final result has stood the test of time and in gaining a Civic Trust Award it was commented that Durham had become 'a richer, safer place'.

NORTHERN ENGLAND

LOCATION from the Millburngate shopping centre cross over Framwellgate Bridge into the historic centre and continue up to the Market Place and into Elvet Street
LOCAL AUTHORITY Durham City Council

Durham City Council and Durham County Council

HULL: MARKET SQUARE

This is an important public space given new life through the closure to traffic and the use of high-quality materials and civic sculpture. The Market Square was redesigned to celebrate the city's 700th anniversary in 1999 largely because the original paving scheme from the early 1980s had become unattractive and unsuitable. That scheme had not excluded traffic from the square, allowed vehicles to cross in a random fashion and created danger for pedestrians. The square was partially occupied by stalls on market days but business had declined because of its distance from the main shopping areas.

The new scheme excluded traffic from the square but access had to be maintained to the parish church so part of King Street, a Georgian thoroughfare built originally in 1771, was reintroduced next to the churchyard. The existing space was relatively large and bare and to make it more intimate, a statue of Andrew Marvell, the 17th-century poet born in Hull, was placed within the space. A second line of trees was introduced on the southern side of the square to link up with a long-term idea to plant trees in the churchyard. The statue was located in the south-east corner of the square to close the corner visually as well as to be next to the Old Grammar School which Marvell had attended. A local artist was commissioned to provide a feature on the northern side of the square where two metal banners identify Hull's association with fishing and ships. More pavement space was provided to accommodate outdoor seating and encourage the emerging café society to develop. Closeby, The Deep, a spectacular new aquarium, is well worth a detour.

LOCATION in the heart of Hull's Old Town Conservation Area on the eastern side of the city centre, to the east of Prince's Dock

LOCAL AUTHORITY Borough of Kingston upon Hull

Borough of Kingston upon Hull

LEEDS: MILLENNIUM SQUARE

A major public space has been provided in the centre of Leeds which was formerly used as a large surface carpark. Millennium Square provides a hub for events immediately next to the Civic Hall and the Civic Theatre. The impressive Civic Hall, built in 1933, forms the major building to which the square relates. The square was conceived as a catalyst for regeneration at the heart of a new civic quarter where residential, leisure, commercial and cultural uses would be added to existing amenities. Technology would be provided to enable the space to be used for public events and entertainment and to repair the urban form of the area which had been adversely affected by previous demolitions. An imaginative new building containing a bar and restaurant with outdoor space on a raised terrace with apartments above overlooks the public space which is frequently used for outdoor performances and television spectaculars. Part of this building accommodates projection facilities in an unusually shaped add-on structure. The public square, paved in natural materials and excellently detailed, slopes down from the Civic Hall towards the Town Hall where a garden sculpture and water feature are included.

Further mixed-use development of two existing buildings forms the south-eastern side of the space and a new community theatre is proposed to complete the square. Adjacent sites have been developed for housing.

LOCATION on the northern side of the city centre, north of The Headrow
LOCAL AUTHORITY Leeds City Council

John Thorp, Civic Architect

LEEDS: THE CALLS

A lively urban quarter has been created in The Calls (the name derives from a medieval word, 'cawl', meaning watercourse), a street about 800 metres to the east of Leeds City station, by opening up barriers that previously made access to the area less inviting. Existing warehouse buildings on the river Aire have been converted to new uses, new housing constructed on available sites and a new pedestrian bridge provides links to the south bank where housing, employment, shopping and restaurants have been opened up. Further to the east is located the Armouries Museum. New bridges, particularly for pedestrian use, have been a feature of regeneration proposals included in a number of waterway developments throughout the country, providing desirable connections to previously separated areas. The Calls' buildings have been imaginatively converted for many uses including offices, a hotel, restaurants and flats.

The Calls is one example of the changes that urban-development corporations – in this case Leeds Development Corporation – were able to achieve within limited time scales. Immediately to the north of The Calls, Cuthbert Brodrick's Corn Exchange of 1861 with its oval space and dome is now used for crafts, cafés and shopping, and includes a performance space.

LOCATION 800 metres to the east of Leeds City station, south of the railway viaduct
LOCAL AUTHORITY Leeds City Council

masterplan Llewelyn-Davies

LEEDS: VICTORIA QUARTER

By far the most sumptuous of arcades in Leeds is County Arcade. Completed in 1904, it was designed by Britain's most prolific theatre architect, Frank Matcham. A Byzantine level of embellishment in terracotta, green-glazed faience, cast iron, mosaics and mahogany is draped over every surface. By the mid-1980s County Arcade was ageing and overlain with plastic and neon shop fascias. The owners, Prudential, decided it was time for a revamp. Their architect chose to continue in Leeds' tradition and also to create a new arcade along adjacent Queen Victoria Street by securing its pedestrianisation and roofing it over in glass. The renamed Victoria Quarter links the office area to the markets and bus station. The new arcade encourages passers-by to linger by protecting them from the elements and wine bars and restaurants spill out into it. By adding contemporary craft objects in sympathy with the original, a chore is transformed into a delight for the senses. Brian Clarke's stained-glass roof to the arcade is unmissable.

The arcades merge into the city fabric and contribute to the area's regeneration. The Quarter has now attracted major retailers and is at the heart of city-centre activity. What a pity that today's fixation with security means that the arcades are closed at certain times.

Close by is the recently converted Corn Exchange with shops and cafés, and The Calls (page 8.12) by the river Aire.

LOCATION from Leeds City station take Boar Lane then go left into Vicar Lane. The Victoria Quarter is to the left
LOCAL AUTHORITY Leeds City Council

Derek Latham & Co Architects

NEWCASTLE UPON TYNE: BYKER

The Byker estate was designed by the architect Ralph Erskine who set up an office in the centre of the redevelopment area and participated with residents in the project. The layout is organised around a pedestrian network which provides a fascinating variety of spaces, including tightly constrained narrow alleyways and intimate courtyards. Parking is mainly confined to the perimeter in order to ensure safe places for children to play and a quiet atmosphere for families. The most celebrated feature is the Byker Wall: a series of long terraces of maisonettes from six to twelve storeys in height which snake their way around the north and east sides of the area. These were designed to exclude the noise from a motorway that was never built and also to provide protection from cold north-easterly winds. The Wall is finished with multi-coloured brickwork in large patterns on the outside, while on the sides facing the sun there are access decks and balconies with balustrading stained in a variety of colours. Although the Wall is the dominant element, the larger part of the area consists of two-storey houses and flats with gardens and balconies which are designed in a variety of forms, materials and colours.

In January 2000 English Heritage included Byker on its list of buildings of architectural and historic interest after the city council threatened to demolish some of the blocks. Byker was awarded the Harvard University Urban Design Award in 1988.

LOCATION on the A187 about 1.6 kilometres east of Newcastle upon Tyne city centre. Metro stop Byker, on the line to the coast
LOCAL AUTHORITY Newcastle upon Tyne City Council

Ralph Erskine

NEWCASTLE UPON TYNE: EAST QUAYSIDE

A masterplan was produced for Newcastle's East Quayside area in about 1990; within this individual architects have worked on particular projects. The area now includes office accommodation, the law courts which were relocated here, private housing and ancillary restaurants, bars and a hotel. The riverside walk and the main street, set back from the water's edge, have created a linear district which is well integrated with the rest of the city. A pedestrian link is provided up Sandgate, celebrated in the traditional song. Considerable attention has been paid to the detail of the public realm and the way in which public art has been integrated in the proposals. Existing buildings have been converted to new uses, such as the Cooperative Warehouse, imaginatively converted to the Malmaison Hotel. A Piano and Pitcher wine bar is located directly on the quayside and behind this Keelman Square provides a further space, enlivened by sculpture, for outdoor dining.

All this is further enhanced by Gateshead's Millennium Bridge (designed by Wilkinson Eyre and Gifford and Partners) opened in summer 2001, a foot- and cycle-bridge that links Newcastle's quayside to Gateshead's where the conversion by Ellis Williams Architects of the Baltic Flour Mills into the Baltic Centre for Contemporary Art and the construction of the Music Centre (Foster and Partners) provide a new vision for the Tyne.

NORTHERN ENGLAND

LOCATION northern side of the Tyne, east of the Tyne Bridge
LOCAL AUTHORITY Newcastle upon Tyne City Council

masterplan Terry Farrell & Partners

NEWCASTLE UPON TYNE: GRAINGER TOWN

Grainger Town provides an immense improvement in the public realm in the centre of Newcastle in terms of pedestrian space and the reintroduction of mixed uses. This part of the city retains the layout and buildings created between 1825 and 1840 by the architect John Dobson, a builder named Richard Grainger, and the town clerk, John Clayton. However, the area had declined particularly through the emergence of new forms of retail and commercial activity and in the early 1990s was exhibiting all the classic symptoms of decay – vacancy, poor maintenance and traffic problems. A regeneration strategy was prepared for the area in order to submit bids for funding and then a detailed urban design framework was prepared for the Grainger Town Partnership, a private company. This focused on Grey's Monument, the Theatre Royal, Market Street and Grainger Street.

A key objective has been derived from the philosophy that streets are for people, giving access for all by improving pedestrian and cycling facilities while striking a balance with legitimate traffic needs. Common elements have been the widening of pavements and the use of quality natural paving materials such as Caithness stone and granite. Street lighting and furniture have been improved and elements of public art have been included to make the area more vibrant.

A further place of interest in the city centre is the 'Blue Carpet' designed by Thomas Heatherwick, adjacent to the Laing Art Gallery.

LOCATION Grainger Street runs north from Central station up to Grey's Monument
LOCAL AUTHORITY Newcastle upon Tyne City Council

Gillespies

SHEFFIELD: PEACE GARDENS

Peace Gardens has been transformed into an exciting, memorable, people-friendly space which attracts hundreds of visitors and residents... raised lawns are a honeypot for picnickers and sunbathers while the fountain attracts young bathers in the summer. The area has become Sheffield's beach.

What was previously an area of soft landscape separated from the adjacent footpath on Pinstone Street has been integrated into the new plans for developing the area to the east of the town hall for retail uses, an hotel, an art gallery and a winter garden. A curved line of paving provides direction for pedestrians and a series of water features steps down to a spectacular grid of fountains attracting people into the space. The success of the public realm can also be measured by the interest taken by private developers including the provision of new flats in a refurbished building overlooking the Peace Gardens.

NORTHERN ENGLAND

LOCATION south of the town hall, east of Pinstone Street
LOCAL AUTHORITY Sheffield City Council

Sheffield Design and Property

SHEFFIELD: VICTORIA QUAYS

Redundant canal buildings and railway structures combine with marina facilities and new development to provide an attractive water space close to the centre of Sheffield. Victoria Quay, including a four-storey warehouse, was opened in 1819 as the terminal of the Sheffield and Tinsley Canal. It was taken over in 1848 by the Manchester Sheffield and Lincolnshire Railway Company and continued in commercial use until 1970. Various ideas for its re-use were proposed over the years but nothing was realised until the Sheffield Urban Development Corporation promoted its development which led to buildings being restored in 1994–95. An hotel, now the Hilton, has been constructed on the eastern side. This uses the railway viaduct for some of its accommodation, including a café and some ancillary shops. The Straddle Warehouse built across the canal in 1895 has been converted to offices and new offices have been constructed on the western side of the basin which now operates as a marina managed by British Waterways. The adjacent Sheaf Quay has been converted to a pub. Public art which reflects the traditions of the area is included on the quays.

Sheffield's light-rail system runs close by the Quays, connecting the city centre to Meadowhall to the east, Hillsborough to the north and Mosborough to the south.

LOCATION access off Furnival Road on the east side of the city centre, north of Park Hill
LOCAL AUTHORITY Sheffield City Council

Sheffield Urban Development Corporation

SUNDERLAND: ST PETER'S RIVERSIDE

About 1.5 kilometres from Sunderland city centre on the banks of the river Wear is one of the showpieces of the former Tyne and Wear Urban Development Corporation. The work of the corporation was instrumental in breathing confidence into an area that had declined alongside the heavy-engineering and shipbuilding industries of the north-east. St Peter's Riverside forms part of the national cycle route, next to the impressive bridges and industrial heritage of the Wear. The heavy use of the riverside cycle route provides both connectivity and activity – the Sustrans route is enhanced by a high standard of public art along the riverside and reconnects the city to the river. The qualities of location and sense of place have attracted the University of Sunderland to establish a residential teaching campus at St Peter's. The National Glass Centre (designed by Andrew Gollifer) has become an important new landmark on the north bank of the river as well as providing a national tourist attraction. The centre demonstrates the potential of glass as building material – linking inside and outside horizontally and vertically. You can go into the restaurant, sit back with your coffee, look out to the city backdrop, bridges and the river and literally look up to the people of the city as they walk over your head.

LOCATION take Fawcett Street north from the main station to North Bridge Street; follow Sustrans signs to the south bank of the Wear and Riverside
LOCAL AUTHORITY Sunderland City Council

Tyne and Wear Urban Development Corporation

WAKEFIELD: KIRKGATE

The shopping area of Kirkgate and the cathedral precinct have been unified by an integrated paving scheme of high quality.

Kirkgate was pedestrianised in the early 1970s and paved with standard concrete slabs. In 1989 the council decided that a total replacement should be undertaken rather than mere repair and it appointed Tess Jaray, an artist and designer who had already been involved in Centenary Square, Birmingham (page 6.8). She responded by redefining the brief and extending its possibilities: 'this was a good opportunity to shape the precincts, to unify the city and the cathedral, thereby giving it the centre it so badly needed'. Crucial to her plan is the integration of the cathedral with the surrounding streets and the creation of an aesthetic unity between the various elements. A low wall and grassy bank along the cathedral's south side were removed and replaced with a sweep of three paved terraces linked by a series of York stone steps. Design motifs are inspired by the cathedral and a simple design of blue paviours repeated against a background of buff paviours in a herringbone pattern makes a subtle reference to the Trinity. On the three terraces the basis of the design is the cross in buff against blue and the cross is also featured in the design of planters. The tracery of the cathedral is repeated in the cast-steel bins, bollards and lighting columns. The section of the pedestrianised area down the sloping street uses a further variation of the buff and blue herringbone paviour pattern with a solid blue central pathway flanked by a line of pleached trees, alluding to the aisle of the cathedral.

LOCATION in the centre of the city to the south of the Bull Ring, adjacent to the Cathedral Church of All Saints
LOCAL AUTHORITY Wakefield City Council

Wakefield City Council and Tess Jaray

YORK: RIVERSIDE

This small development shows what can be done to use the benefits of a riverside location coupled with the re-use of existing buildings. The City Screen Cinema is an imaginative adaptation of the former Yorkshire Herald building which, together with new structures, provides a three-screen cinema and – tucked alongside or on adjacent sites – three restaurants and bars. A series of public spaces has been created along the riverside, partly by cantilevered boardwalks, giving new views along the river and making an important contribution to the city's revitalisation. The scheme lies just behind St Martin's church on Coney Street, identified by the projecting clock on the street frontage.

The centre of York is a case study in how to provide good facilities for the pedestrian in a honeypot visitor location. Stonegate, which leads to the minster, was paved, appropriately in York stone, as part of Architectural Heritage Year in 1975 and this paving has been extended to other parts of the city centre. The continuation of Stonegate towards the river, St Helen's Square, also now pedestrianised, provides a popular location for street performances.

LOCATION north side of the river with access off Coney Street close to the Guildhall
LOCAL AUTHORITY York City Council

Panter Hudspith Architects

YORK: ST MARY'S SQUARE

An informal and lively place enhanced by the retention of a mature tree and its relationship to St Mary's church. The space was created in 1984 as part of the Coppergate development and it provides a connection to various pedestrian routes to other parts of the city centre. The enclosure of the square is achieved by a series of buildings at different angles to each other, creating a space which is both informal and lively. Although there are changes from the small-scale pedestrian street of shops (with residential accommodation above) to the larger scale of the square itself, the spaces retain a human proportion. This is helped by the glazed canopy that surrounds the space and gives shelter to shoppers and visitors. A large old horse-chestnut tree has been retained in the centre of the square with new tree planting next to it adding a human scale and informality to the space.

The Yorvik Viking Centre within the Coppergate development creates large queues which encircle the square during holiday periods. The space is usually busy with buskers, music and an outdoor café. It is also worth walking along Stonegate. It is one of the main approaches to the minster and one of the city's finest streets, with many Georgian and Victorian shopfronts, some masking medieval structures. It was closed to traffic in 1971 after a campaign by the Civic Society.

NORTHERN ENGLAND

LOCATION south-west of Parliament Street with access off Coppergate
LOCAL AUTHORITY York City Council

Chapman Taylor Partners

SCOTLAND

INTRODUCTION 9.2
DUNDEE: PEDESTRIAN AREA 9.4
EDINBURGH: THE ROYAL MILE 9.6
EDINBURGH: THE WATER OF LEITH 9.8
GLASGOW: BUCHANAN STREET 9.10
GLASGOW: CATHEDRAL PRECINCT 9.12
GLASGOW: ITALIAN CENTRE 9.14
GLASGOW: ROYAL EXCHANGE SQUARE 9.16
HAMILTON: TOWN SQUARE 9.18
IRVINE: HARBOURSIDE 9.20
KILMARNOCK: TOWN CENTRE 9.22
LEITH: WATERFRONT 9.24

INTRODUCTION

Scotland's main area of population is centred on the Clyde and Forth rivers and their hinterlands – what Sir Patrick Geddes termed 'Clydeforth'. Edinburgh was christened the 'Athens of the North' due to the impact of Calton Hill with its Greek-revival buildings and the partly built Parthenon. This closes the vista at the end of Princes Street, the open side of which looks south towards the castle and the Old Town silhouetted on the ridge. The spine of the Old Town is formed by the Royal Mile (page 9.6) which connects the castle along High Street through Lawnmarket past the Cathedral of St Giles and Canongate to Holyrood Palace and the new parliament. Many of the houses and wynds off High Street are 17th century or earlier. Housing the growing population led to the development of the New Town, connected to the Old Town by the North Bridge. A competition for its layout was won by James Craig in 1766; his scheme centred on the higher land on George Street with a square at each end – Charlotte Square retains its original character. Moray Place, another delightful space created in Craig's plan, is close to Queen Street Gardens which provide the largest of the green lungs within the layout. The Water of Leith (page 9.8) meanders through the area to the north of the New Town, emerging at the waterside in Leith, Edinburgh's port, revitalised by warehouse conversions, new housing and offices (page 9.24).

Outside Edinburgh, Haddington is a gracious town with wide streets and an attractive town house. In the Borders, Kelso has a wide cobbled square considered by Walter Scott to be the most beautiful in Scotland. North of Edinburgh, Fife has some attractive villages, many of which, including Ceres and Crail, have benefited from the National Trust for Scotland's 'Small Houses' scheme. Culross, to the west, is another fine example of that initiative.

In the east, Dundee, Perth, Aberdeen and Inverness each has its own character.

Dundee has a revitalised centre (page 9.4) and Aberdeen, the granite city, its attractive Castlegate.

On the west side of the country, the dredging of the Clyde enabled Glasgow to become a major industrial and commercial city. It grew rapidly during the industrial revolution and became a major centre for shipbuilding, heavy engineering and trade. Many of the tenements of that period were replaced by peripheral estates or high-rise blocks from the 1960s to the 1980s. The structure of the central city still retains the clarity of the Victorian layout, seen particularly in the Merchant City (page 9.14), Buchanan Street (page 9.10) and parts of Sauchiehall Street and Argyle Street which have been pedestrianised. The riverside provides a potentially pleasant walkway leading eventually to the new Conference Centre (Foster & Partners) linked to the Science Centre across the Clyde. New approaches to housing can be seen in the Gorbals area where the Crown Street regeneration scheme demonstrates that city-scale housing can be provided in a way that meets the demands of all sizes of household. The recent Homes for the Future development north-west of Glasgow Green involves a range of architects on a smaller site to provide diversity.

One of many new communities, Inveraray on the west coast, the seat of the Dukes of Argyll, was rebuilt as a small town in the 18th century using a formal layout. New Lanark, south-east of Glasgow on the banks of the Clyde, was founded in 1784 as a successful experiment in building a new community based on the mill and providing social benefits for employees. Scotland's five post-war new towns are very different, catering for a much higher population and range of employment. Cumbernauld is an innovative approach to developing around a hilltop in the central belt, while Irvine on the Clyde coast (page 9.20) benefited from its river and coastal setting. The other new towns – East Kilbride, Glenrothes and Livingston – have succeeded in attracting a range of employment.

DUNDEE: PEDESTRIAN AREA

Dundee's High Street formed the original medieval heart of the city and retains much of its irregular plan, intimate character and core functions. In the early 20th century it was supplemented with the more formal and grand City Square which now forms the southern termination of the Georgian vista down Reform Street. In the 1990s this whole area was completely refurbished to provide a pedestrian environment using a range of natural materials and incorporating innovative artworks. Three new focal points have been formed in the area: outside Arnotts and the Clydesdale Bank at the end of Murraygate; at the junction of High Street and City Square; and outside Boots where a quiet oasis has been created. The resulting scheme won the 1998 Town Centre Environment Award. Contributing to this success has been the use of high-quality materials including Caithness stone, granite and whin (a dark basaltic rock), and the introduction of street furniture commissioned from local artists. A unique feature is a 'life-sized' bronze dragon forming the focus of a space in the High Street. These works have been complemented by the restoration of historic frontages and the development of contemporary buildings to create one of the most attractive city-centre environments in Scotland.

LOCATION take the covered walkway from Dundee station to Nethergate and High Street
LOCAL AUTHORITY Dundee City Council

Gillespies

EDINBURGH: THE ROYAL MILE

The Royal Mile is Edinburgh's most historic street and the public realm has been improved by new ground surfaces and street furniture. Pavements, road surfaces and street furniture have been replaced with high-quality materials and traffic has been banned from some areas, providing an appropriate setting for important civic and national buildings.

The designers described The Royal Mile as 'a meandering river of city life – adjusted, dignified and monumentalised by a classical overlay with its medieval underlay of closes and wynds... The activity of the street is a brilliant cacophony... The majority of the buildings are ordinary, working simply together to achieve richness, a sense of history and a special place... The brief was to widen the footpath, to accommodate the pedestrian, to reduce the impact of vehicles while allowing them to continue where essential.'

The proposal was to be seen to be doing as little as possible and not to design a 'Royal Mile style'. Black Caithness stone was selected for the floor surfaces – 'the stone is magical and when it rains, it smiles!' Stone was traditionally used in most Scottish cities until it was replaced by concrete in the post-war years. The redesign uses stone in many forms for setts, kerbs and paving. In places the road is raised to pedestrian level with simple elements used to define spaces. These can be removed for ceremonies and performances.

SCOTLAND

LOCATION in the Old Town running from Edinburgh Castle to Holyrood House
LOCAL AUTHORITY Edinburgh City Council

Page & Park Architects in association with Ian White Associates

EDINBURGH: THE WATER OF LEITH

The Water of Leith Walkway traverses architectural configurations and landmarks of central Edinburgh and is a remarkable corridor, giving the contemporary a presence rivalling that of the historic. At Roseburn, willows mingle with the waterside architects' studios as the Walkway passes under Coltbridge Viaduct. Further on, a wide meadow forms the foreground to the classical façade of the Gallery of Modern Art in the former merchant school (William Burn, 1928). Across Belford Road is Thomas Hamilton's baroque set-piece of 1833; reopened in March 1999 after conversion by Terry Farrell as the Dean Gallery for Surrealism, Dadaism and the work of Eduardo Paolozzi. Paths link the galleries to the Walkway at Bells Brae as Dean Bridge (Thomas Telford, 1832) soars overhead. A path follows alongside bluebell woods below Moray Place. The Walkway continues to Stockbridge, passing 19th-century workers' colony houses near the Botanic Gardens and the striking conversion of the former Stockbridge Tollhouse into a riverside restaurant, designed by Malcolm Fraser Architects. At Canonmills, the dome of the Standard Life building marks an outcrop of modern serviced premises spilling out from the New Town.

This is one of those rare places where no single designer can be identified as taking the lead or preparing a masterplan but it shows how good designers can respond to a special location.

LOCATION to walk or cycle the Walkway you will need a gazetteer of Edinburgh which indicates off-road routes
LOCAL AUTHORITY Edinburgh City Council

GLASGOW: BUCHANAN STREET

Work on the southern section of Buchanan Street involved the replacement of unsatis-factory brick paviours while in the northern section the completion of the Buchanan Galleries adjacent to the concert hall provides the total street scene envisaged in earlier plans. The design is the result of a competition won by Gillespies working in association with MBM of Barcelona. It emphasises the clarity of the form of Buchanan Street by removing clutter and revealing the richness and elegance of its architecture. New columns of light ranged along the eastern side of the street identify a zone for cafés, canopies and performance spaces. The geometry of the lighting columns is reinforced in the way the surface of the street is paved in natural stone; a window-shopping zone runs along the east and west sides of the street leaving a central passage for service access. The Buchanan Galleries have a large Habitat store. Its first-floor restaurant provides a good view of the scurrying pedestrians.

It is well worth visiting Princes Square in the southern part of Buchanan Street. Here an internal courtyard has been transformed to provide a three-storey atrium space with a diverse range of uses. The Lighthouse, Glasgow's design centre, is located on a pedestrian way off the west side of this part of the street.

LOCATION north–south street to the east of Central station running between Argyle Street and Sauchiehall Street
LOCAL AUTHORITY Glasgow City Council

Gillespies

GLASGOW: CATHEDRAL PRECINCT

An unsatisfactory approach to the cathedral previously split up by roads has been transformed into a meaningful place using street furniture, planting and appropriate materials.

In 1984 the city council held a competition to produce ideas for improving the setting of the cathedral, whose civic prominence had been adversely affected over the years by the way the Royal Infirmary had increased its development on the adjacent site. The winning scheme sought to extend the open space around the cathedral and the adjoining necropolis towards Castle Street. These became pedestrian spaces and the means of approaching the cathedral. Alongside this on the southern side a new visitor centre has been constructed in a Scottish vernacular style more in keeping with the Provand's Lodgings, an historic building on Castle Street. The general objective of the new layout was to develop some relationship not only with the cathedral but also with the infirmary. A series of trees and seats define the edge of the approach to the cathedral and artist Jack Sloan designed a number of features within the scheme including the lighting columns.

Do not forget to visit the amazing necropolis set on an adjacent hill.

SCOTLAND

LOCATION on the eastern side of the city centre at the end of Cathedral Street where it joins Castle Street
LOCAL AUTHORITY Glasgow City Council

Page & Park Architects in association with Ian White Associates

GLASGOW: ITALIAN CENTRE

The Italian Centre is the result of the conversion of a classical building originally containing shops and warehouses into a complex of shops, restaurants, offices and flats – a mix of uses that would promote Italian goods and design and also evoke to some extent the culture and atmosphere of Italy. The exterior façades were retained and enhanced by plinths and new elements and a main entrance placed on John Street with an inner courtyard used almost as an Italian piazza. The façades of the courtyard are all treated individually and reflect the walkway that runs around three sides. A large bay is occupied by one of the restaurants and within this space the levels are used imaginatively, including water and sculpture. The artists involved in the project included Shona Kinloch, Jack Sloan and Sandy Stoddart. Although the courtyard is closed outside trading hours the centre makes a positive contribution to the regeneration of this part of Glasgow, known as The Merchant City.

SCOTLAND

LOCATION south-east of George Square fronting on to Cochrane Street, John Street and Ingram Street
LOCAL AUTHORITY Glasgow City Council

Page & Park Architects

GLASGOW: ROYAL EXCHANGE SQUARE

This is an urban-design set piece vastly improved by the removal of most traffic and the use of high-quality paving materials and street furniture.

In 1995 Gillespies devised a new public-realm strategy for Glasgow city centre. The second demonstration project was the redesign of Royal Exchange Square, probably the most elegant example of urban design in the city. The Royal Exchange was originally the site of a merchant's mansion and garden which was remodelled to provide the city's new exchange building and around which the square was laid out. It was converted to a public library in the 1950s and became the city's Gallery of Modern Art in 1996 when the space around it was repaved as a pedestrian-priority area, the key principle being to restrict the use of vehicles to taxis, cycles, service and emergency vehicles. The space was extensively redesigned with the concept of 'a gallery within a gallery', emphasis being placed on a simple elegant treatment and the use of quality materials. Traditional Caithness flagstones were used with Cornish grey granite steps; the footpath around the gallery was raised by two steps to provide a plinth for the display of outdoor exhibits while protecting the gallery's basement area. A smooth continuous area has been created in front of the shops and restaurants to encourage use as an outdoor eating space. A range of street furniture was designed for exclusive use in the square. The gallery and buildings around the square have been floodlit and rows of uplighters supplement this lighting.

LOCATION east of Buchanan Street on the axis of Ingram Street
LOCAL AUTHORITY Glasgow City Council

Gillespies

HAMILTON: TOWN SQUARE

As part of an extension to Hamilton's central area it was decided to create a town square as a civic focus, to provide a public performance area and connect this to other parts of the centre that were being pedestrianised.

After a number of years of decline, in 1994 the council launched a 'Hamilton Ahead Initiative' to regenerate and revitalise the town centre. A strategy was prepared for the whole area which included the provision of a town square as the centrepiece of the new Hamilton. Part of the strategy involved a new food store on the edge of the town centre together with a retail park and a multiscreen cinema. The Asda store forms one edge to the town square and includes a restaurant and coffee shop. A continuation of the building steps up the hill and includes offices and shopping units.

The square is on three main levels with the intermediate level partly covered with a tented structure and providing seating for events. Public art, stainless-steel seating and lighting combine to provide an imaginative identity for the main lower-level space. Paving is laid out in circles with a light line running through the space and being pulled upwards by an athletic figure designed by David Annand. The eastern edge to the square is formed by a sculptural screen wall with a motif using the concept of a filmstrip. The lower space is regularly used for art and craft fairs and other events organised through the town centre manager. The western edge to the square is being redeveloped for mixed uses including residential on the upper floors. The southern edge is intended for a leisure building.

SCOTLAND

LOCATION north-east side of town centre, next to Asda
LOCAL AUTHORITY South Lanarkshire District Council

Ferguson McIlveen

IRVINE: HARBOURSIDE

Sensitive new development has enhanced the environmental qualities of a waterside setting. Irvine served Glasgow and its hinterland as a port in the time of Robert Burns but its historic harbour had lost most of the original buildings by the time Irvine Development Corporation was established under the New Towns Act in 1968. Sensitive infill development was originally carried out in the 1970s together with the building of a leisure centre and the reclamation of derelict land to form a beach park. However, the existence of a nearby quay handling Nobel's explosives prevented further development until this use ended, after which extensive additional housing could be added to the area. New housing along the harbour front designed by the development corporation defines a hard edge and at the same time provides a sophisticated articulation including Mackintosh-inspired details. The harbourside is enlivened by pubs, the Harbour Arts Centre, crafts workshops, a watersports centre and a maritime museum. Housing extends behind the frontage to enable more people to enjoy the adjacent facilities.

A new facility – The Big Idea – has been developed on the Ardeer site, accessible across a footbridge from the Irvine side of the river. This tells the story of Nobel's inventions and other inventors.

LOCATION west of Irvine town centre and the station. Parking is available by the beach park
LOCAL AUTHORITY North Ayrshire District Council

Irvine Development Corporation

KILMARNOCK: TOWN CENTRE

The pedestrianisation of Kilmarnock's main street, King Street, is a classic example of how to improve a local shopping environment.

What was once heavily used by traffic is now an attractive people-friendly oasis enabling people to enjoy shopping without pollution and danger. High-quality materials, carefully rethought street furniture and the joyful inclusion of street sculpture provide essential lessons in what can so easily become tawdry, cut-price exercises in the exclusion of vehicles. A central space provides a location for major sculpture, a visual connection to the Laigh Kirk, an historic building, and the re-use of a landmark bank building as a surprising outlet for Ladbrokes!

The pedestrianisation of King Street formed one part of the regeneration project for Kilmarnock which also included the rebuilding of the central bus station and the restoration of the Laigh Kirk. The three elements have created a new civic presence for the town. Shona Kinloch's sculptures of heads and animals add a distinct sense of humour to the normal shopping experience. The scheme won the major Civic Trust Award for 1997.

LOCATION King Street, centre of the shopping area
LOCAL AUTHORITY East Ayrshire Council

Page & Park Architects in association with Ian White Associates

LEITH: WATERFRONT

Until the mid 1980s Leith and its docks were considered an area into which no respectable Edinburgher would venture. Certainly the idea of Leith being a place to visit in the evening would be met with incredulity. This changed with an initiative by the then Scottish Development Agency and the Forth Ports plc. A masterplan was prepared by Conran Roche.

The plan focused on an area defined by Commercial Street and The Shore which fronts the Water of Leith. One of the important elements of the masterplan was infrastructure provision including floorscape improvements. The cobbled streets and restored classical façades reminiscent of Amsterdam, together with chic street lights and pavement cafés, create a Mediterranean-style setting romantic enough to soften the hardest of hearts. A striking new Ocean Terminal shopping centre has been built.

In particular, the conversion works provided a setting for the refurbishment of the old MacDonald and Muir bonded warehouse which now – as Commercial Quay – accommodates bars and restaurants, specialist shops, offices and housing.

Along Commercial Street new offices and housing bring life to the area and provide a good example of mixed-use development. The future success of the area will depend on how many people come to shop and see the former royal yacht 'Britannia' when its refurbishment is complete, and on the workers in the new Scottish Executive forsaking Princes Street for the delights of a waterside setting and a new shopping experience.

LOCATION from Edinburgh city centre, a bus ride down Leith Walk to Bernard Street and the former Corn Exchange brings one within a short walk of The Shore
LOCAL AUTHORITY Edinburgh City Council

masterplan Conran Roche

IRELAND

INTRODUCTION 10.2
ARMAGH: THE MARKET PLACE 10.4
BELFAST: LANYON PLACE 10.6
CORK: EMMET PLACE 10.8
DONEGAL: THE DIAMOND 10.10
DUBLIN: THE CAMPSHIRES 10.12
DUBLIN CASTLE: DUBH LINN GARDEN 10.14
DUBLIN: TEMPLE BAR SQUARE 10.16
DUBLIN: MEETING HOUSE SQUARE 10.18
DUBLIN: SMITHFIELD 10.20
DUN LAOGHAIRE: FERRY TERMINAL PIAZZA 10.22
PORTLAOISE: FITZMAURICE PLACE 10.24
WATERFORD: JOHN ROBERTS SQUARE 10.26

INTRODUCTION

Dublin – the major urban centre for the whole of Ireland – has a rich tradition in letters, the arts and sciences. The capital and seat of the government of the Irish Republic, Dublin's great architectural period was in the 18th century when it was the second city of the British Empire – a city of fine public buildings, elegant streets and squares. This can still be seen in Georgian Merrion Square and Fitzwilliam Square and in the layout of Trinity College, strategically located in the centre of the city. However, the shift in political and economic status following the Act of Union of 1800 meant that major building projects gradually ceased. Compared with, for example, Belfast, the city became an architectural backwater. Independence in 1922 ushered in state programmes of building in the fields of housing, education and health. The growth of the city (which now houses about one third of the republic's population) took the form of outward expansion and much of Georgian Dublin survived relatively intact although needing restoration. The tentative beginnings of urban regeneration in the 1970s flowered into a programme of integrated area plans for large-scale redevelopment. The Dublin Docklands Development Authority was established to coordinate the redevelopment of that area and Temple Bar, begun in the 1990s, became an outstanding example of culturally led regeneration (pages 10.16 and 10.18). Ongoing urban-design initiatives include the creation of a civic thoroughfare from the medieval city through Westmoreland Street and O'Connell Street.

Cork is the second largest city in the Irish Republic, a city served by water, with its heart on an island between two arms of the river Lee. Extensive improvements are being carried out to restore the city's historic buildings and preserve its character. Limerick, the city described in *Angela's Ashes*, lies mainly to the east of the Shannon and until recently turned its back on the river which is its best asset; new developments relate themselves to the river and its open spaces. Other towns worth visiting including Wexford, a vibrant town, Waterford with its Georgian heritage, Westport, laid out by James Wyatt in the 1770s, Galway where the older parts of the town have been reanimated, and Kilkenny with its fine historic buildings, also noted for its design centre.

Belfast was the only city in Ireland to experience the full effect of the industrial revolution – it became a centre for the shipbuilding, ropemaking and tobacco industries. The wealth produced is reflected in robust buildings of the 19th and early-20th-centuries such as the opera house, Queen's University, the City Hall and St Anne's Cathedral. The Troubles and the decline of traditional industries drastically affected the economy and much of this has been offset by the work of the Laganside Corporation in using redundant land for new activities and broadening the economy.

In the 17th century, Londonderry, originally and still known as Derry, was the site of a major Plantation project organised by the London livery companies – hence its prefix. It was laid out in accordance with Renaissance principles around a square, the Diamond. The old walls are well preserved and provide a walk around most of the city. Armagh, considered the religious capital of Ireland, includes two dominant cathedrals both dedicated to St Patrick. Its layout reflects the ditches that once ringed the earliest church, founded in 455. Carrickfergus on the north coast grew up around the massive castle begun in 1180; its adjacent industrial harbour has now been redeveloped for leisure uses and to provide a marina.

ARMAGH: THE MARKET PLACE

An important historic location is enhanced by an excellent new theatre and arts centre which strengthens the sense of place in the centre of Armagh.

The historic centre of the city lies on a steeply sloping hill topped by St Patrick's Cathedral (founded in 455). Below the cathedral the land slopes down to the main shopping street, above which an earlier arts centre was located. This was destroyed by a terrorist bomb in the 1980s. The design for the new arts centre was chosen through an international competition. The new building, known as The Market Place, set out to complete the enclosure to the main public square. Rather than compete for prominence with the tower of the cathedral, the building is tucked into the hillside. This means that the glazed walls of the main pedestrian entrance and the bar and restaurant areas, spectacularly lit at night, form one of the edges to the public space within which an historic celtic cross is located. The other edges to the space are formed by a stepped three-storey terrace of traditional houses and the classical-revival Municipal Technical School, now reused as the city's library. The arts centre includes a 400-seat main auditorium, a 150-seat studio theatre, studios, a gallery and workshops.

The history of Armagh is displayed in the adjacent St Patrick's Trian Centre. This also provides parking off Market Street, some of which is pedestrianised.

IRELAND

LOCATION in the centre of Armagh off Market Street and adjacent to the Trian Centre
LOCAL AUTHORITY Armagh City and District Council

Glenn Howells Architects

BELFAST: LANYON PLACE

The area adjacent to the Waterfront Hall at Lanyon Place provides access to the riverside overlooked by bars and restaurants which serve the concert hall's various uses.

The Laganside Corporation was set up by the government in 1989 to regenerate redundant land and buildings in Belfast's derelict docklands. Many sites – such as Clarendon Dock and the Odyssey site – have been opened up for development, but a number have become single-use areas without becoming part of the city structure for use by everyone. By contrast, Lanyon Place provides a unique forum within the city. By combining an attractive waterside setting with open space it forms a vital focus for the city's public festivals and outdoor performances. A further focus of activity being constructed within this area next to Queens Bridge is a three-storey bar, restaurant and leisure development with terraced public areas overlooking the river. The circular Waterfront Hall designed by Robinson & McIlwaine Architects provides a simple building form enlivened by glazed bars and foyers. A major open space has been created at the heart of the development to provide a dramatic connection between the city centre and the river. It has been designed to respond to three elements: a threshold, a more formal area and the waterfront. The threshold forms the main pedestrian entrance to the site adjacent to Oxford Street and is identified by gateway elements. The main body of the square is designed as uncluttered space and rises to a high point at its centre which links with the café terrace in the Waterfront Hall. The waterfront space is terraced down towards the river and the riverside promenade.

LOCATION on Oxford Street on an axis with Chichester Street adjacent to the west bank of the river Lagan
LOCAL AUTHORITY Belfast City Council

landscape design Camlin Lonsdale Landscape Architects

CORK: EMMET PLACE

Emmet Place is a significant urban space in the historic part of the city of Cork, lying to the south of the river Lee and defined by important civic buildings – the Crawford Art Gallery and Cork Opera House. The space has recently been refurbished, with substantial investment in the public realm and significant changes to both the opera house and the gallery.

Refurbishment of Emmet Place had its genesis in the Cork Historic Area Action Plan, prepared by Urban Initiatives. The strategy identified the twin anchors of Mardyke Place and Emmet Place as establishing the potential for a visitor and leisure spine running east–west through the historic area of the city. Traffic at Emmet Place is now restricted to one lane northwards, allowing the creation of a large pedestrian-friendly area. The refurbishment work included repaving, new lighting, street furniture and tree planting.

The Crawford Art Gallery is one of Cork's most important public buildings. The older part of the structure dates from 1724 and was the city's custom house until 1818. In 1996 a competition for the design of a new extension was won by Erik van Egeraat Associated Architects. This scheme left the current front building façade untouched and added accommodation on Half Moon Street expressed as a curved brick façade with a transparent lower storey. At one end of Emmet Place the original opera house was burned down in 1955 and a replacement building was designed by Michael Scott. The form and façade of this building became contentious with many of the public; recent refurbishment has given the front façade a more civic presence.

LOCATION south of Lavitt's Quay, east of the Christy Ring Bridge
LOCAL AUTHORITY Cork City Council

Cork City Council

DONEGAL: THE DIAMOND

The Market Square or Diamond, the name generally used in Ulster, is Donegal's focal point. It is a triangular space surrounded by impressive two- and three-storey mixed-use buildings of a type traditionally found in Irish towns. Donegal is a busy market and tourist town and the hub of important communication routes – north, south, east and west. The Diamond had become a busy and bustling place, particularly during the summer months, with conflict between local traffic, through traffic and tourist coaches, as well as being the main parking place in the town. The International Fund for Ireland, established in the wake of the Anglo-Irish Agreement in the mid 1980s, provided funds for urban development and improvement. The fund grant-aided the development of off-street car parking and improvements to the Diamond, including the removal of parking and the creation of a new pedestrian area. Initially, there was considerable opposition from local traders. However, grant-awarding bodies can often achieve things which would otherwise not be implemented. In recent years the through traffic has been removed and the town centre now caters mostly for local and tourist traffic.

The central pedestrian area is an important feature in the town, as a venue for meetings and concerts and is much used and appreciated by shoppers and tourists alike. The high quality of the paving and the general detailing contribute to its overall character and long-term sustainability.

LOCATION central Donegal
LOCAL AUTHORITY Donegal County Council

Donegal County Council

DUBLIN: THE CAMPSHIRES

The Campshires are linear amenity spaces on Dublin's north and south quays, completed from the Custom House to Spencer Dock. They act as an urban greenway making the banks of the river Liffey enjoyable places on which to sit out, walk and cycle. On the northern quay this space provides a unified foreground to riverside elevations of the redeveloped docklands area, enlivened by public art and new glazed pavilions axially related to the adjacent residential development. The improvement to the quays consists of repaving, tree planting, the provision of a cycle route, seating and public art.

The Liffey provides an important lung for the centre of the city. In the 18th century sailing ships used the river up as far as Parliament Street Bridge; further bridges were subsequently added as the shipping trade changed. It is now intended to add a further bridge, a pivoting structure designed by Santiago Calatrava connecting the Campshires on the north bank with the Royal Canal Dock area to the south. Other changes to the Liffey have occurred on the north bank between O'Connell and Grattan Bridges where a cantilevered structure, 'The Boardwalk', has provided a pedestrian route separate from the existing footpath with benches set against the sunny granite quay wall.

However, the highlight of this section is the Millennium Bridge, designed by Howley Harrington Architects, a new pedestrian route crossing the Liffey and linking into Eustace Street in Temple Bar.

LOCATION north bank of the Liffey running east from the Custom House
LOCAL AUTHORITY Dublin Corporation

Dublin Docklands Development Authority

DUBLIN CASTLE: DUBH LINN GARDEN

Dubh Linn Garden is part of the Dublin Castle complex. An oasis of calm away from the bustle of the city, it also gives access to the Chester Beatty Library. Dublin Castle was for centuries the centre of British rule in Ireland. It is a large complex of buildings and open spaces in the historic centre of the city, with fabric above ground dating back to the 13th century and below ground remains of Viking and early-medieval Dublin. The buildings primarily date from the 18th and 19th centuries. The castle is one of a number of large institutional complexes within the centre of Dublin which have historically been relatively inaccessible to the public. By virtue of their use, size, location, and impermeability, they have restricted easy connections between different parts of the city. The opening up of the castle has been a gradual process assisted by work carried out as part of Ireland's preparations for its European Union presidency in 1990. The Chester Beatty Library, which holds a magnificent collection of Asian and oriental manuscripts and artefacts, has been relocated in the castle complex. It also has a small roof garden, open to the public – something rare in Dublin. The library overlooks a large circular lawn which incorporates an interlocking serpent design. The four corners of the space are devoted to smaller themed gardens.

Future plans, made in conjunction with Dublin Corporation, will see a permanent public route passing east–west through the complex. The grounds have matured since the early 1990s and now provide a calm and relatively hidden garden retreat within the bustling city. When the future cross route is introduced, an impenetrable and somewhat unloved part of Dublin will become a significant amenity in a city increasingly in need of such 'soft' public spaces.

LOCATION south of Dame Street and Dame Lane
LOCAL AUTHORITY Dublin Corporation

Office of Public Works

DUBLIN: TEMPLE BAR SQUARE

Temple Bar is an outstanding example of culturally led regeneration. An area that was to have been developed as a bus station has been transformed with a thriving mix of buildings for public uses, restaurants, bars, shops and housing. The principal components of Group 91 Architects' winning scheme for the development were the creation of new public spaces and buildings, the establishment of a strong east–west pedestrian route through the centre of the quarter, the integration of a mix of cultural, commercial and residential uses, and the linking of Temple Bar into the rest of the city on a north–south axis. The two major spaces within the area are Temple Bar Square and Meeting House Square (page 10.18). The former is a new public space on the main route from the southern part of the city centre to the Ha'penny Bridge. It is also the key space on the east–west route through Temple Bar along Essex Street. It simply provides people with an outdoor room which acts as a backdrop to the lively culture which gives the whole district its character. The site – formally a carpark – offered the opportunity to provide a layer of development of varying depth against existing properties. Retail and café uses occupy the ground level and nine residential units are located at the upper levels on the south-western side where the site depth was greater. The square is designed as a level space finished in quartzite with steps along the northern side taking up the slope in the site. The steps are used as informal seating and a line of trees also defines that side of the square. Three lighting masts located on the western side are reflected by stainless-steel bollards on the east. The square is used for a book market at weekends and band recitals are often held there.

LOCATION at junction of Temple Bar and Crown Alley which runs through the area from Dame Street through Merchants Arch to the Ha'penny Bridge
LOCAL AUTHORITY Dublin Corporation

Group 91 Architects (Grafton Architects)

DUBLIN: MEETING HOUSE SQUARE

Meeting House Square is the second major space provided in the Temple Bar area (see page 10.16). It forms part of the sequence of urban spaces running from Temple Bar Square through Cecilia Street to the new Curved Street, on through the arched entrance on Eustace Street to Meeting House Square and out on to Essex Street East. It is essentially an outdoor room around which are gathered the Ark, the Children's Museum, the Irish Film Centre, the Photographic Archive and a mixed-use building. It is at its best when used for a Saturday market, events such as July's European jazz concert or film evenings when visitors can also enjoy using the adjacent restaurants and bars.

The square, formerly used for parking, takes its name from the earlier use of adjacent buildings – the Presbyterian Meeting House and the Quaker Meeting Hall which was transformed in 1992 into the Irish Film Centre. 'The Ark' Children's Cultural Centre, designed by Shane O'Toole and Michael Kelly, has an outdoor stage facing on to the new square. The Irish Film Centre, designed by O'Donnell and Tuomey, has large windows overlooking the square and also provides the screen on to which films are projected. The mixed-use building on the western side of the square, designed by Paul Keogh Architects, contains retail, bar and restaurant space with the Gaiety School of Acting occupying the top two floors. The ground-floor restaurant with its outdoor sitting space and awnings provides the essential everyday life to the square. The design of the square by Paul Keogh Architects complements its cultural uses by providing stage lighting and a circle of uplighters set within the space together with a line of trees.

LOCATION Temple Bar between Eustace Street, Essex Street East and Sycamore Street Square

LOCAL AUTHORITY Dublin Corporation

Group 91 Architects (Paul Keogh Architects)

DUBLIN: SMITHFIELD

Smithfield – a vast elongated cobbled space to the west of the Smithfield Village project – was established by Dublin Corporation in 1665 as a free market for the 'sale of hay, straw, horses and cattle'. It remained Dublin's main outdoor market until the cattle market moved to the outer city in 1863, when decline set in. It later suffered the closure of the distillery on its east side, and its most recent use was as a carpark. The fruit and vegetable market is still located to the east. Despite physical and economic decline over many years, Smithfield managed to maintain a very powerful sense of place and identity due to its essential qualities of scale, proportion, orientation and texture. In 1997 Dublin Corporation promoted an international competition to establish Smithfield as 'the civic space for Dublin for the 21st century'. The winning scheme creates an appropriate scale by the insertion of twelve 26-metre-high masts which support lights, reflectors, gas braziers and PA equipment. The line of masts reinforces the length of Smithfield and establishes a relationship with the distillery chimney that remains as part of the Smithfield Village development. Character is established by materials – mainly granite setts with a new pattern of inlaid diagonal flags giving scale to the area and providing a smooth surface across the space.

The eastern edge to the space is formed by Smithfield Village, a mixed-use development designed by A & D Wejchert woven around and over remains of part of the old Jameson's Distillery. A whiskey visitor centre, a traditional Irish music centre, Chief O'Neill's Hotel, a Children's Court and a wide range of residential accommodation interact to provide interesting and varied spaces within the large scale development. For visitors, the only accessible viewing tower in the city is provided above the retained distillery chimney.

LOCATION north of the Liffey, 1.2 kilometres west of O'Connell Street
LOCAL AUTHORITY Dublin Corporation

McGarry Ni Eanaigh Architects

DUN LAOGHAIRE: FERRY TERMINAL PIAZZA

The piazza was created as an integral part of a new development serving the ferry terminal. The ferry port is located within Dun Laoghaire Harbour – an early-19th-century development designed by Sir John Rennie. Of significant architectural and historic importance, it ranks high among Europe's great historic harbours. The piazza, close to the centre of Dun Laoghaire, has become a popular civic space and provides an attractive entry and departure point to and from Ireland. It is, in addition, much used by local people for musical events and similar gatherings.

The terminal, designed by Burke Kennedy Doyle Architects, has a maritime flavour and makes a significant contribution to Dun Laoghaire. A feature of the piazza is the sculpture by Eamon O'Doherty, a leading Irish artist, reflecting the sailing tradition of the area. The piazza has almost a Barcelona feeling with the sinuous Gaudiesque mosaic seat by Orla Kaminski and Laura O'Hagan providing an important visual element.

LOCATION Dun Laoghaire Harbour close to the Dart station linking to central Dublin
LOCAL AUTHORITY Dun Laoghaire and Rathdown County Council

urban design Mitchell & Associates

PORTLAOISE: FITZMAURICE PLACE

Fitzmaurice Place is a newly developed civic space on the edge of the historic centre of Portlaoise, a busy regional centre and county town almost 100 kilometres south-west of Dublin. Fitzmaurice Place evolved from an urban-renewal scheme which provided for a mixture of residential and commercial uses on what was previously derelict and under-used land. It is a good example of what can be achieved through 'planning gain'. The developer constructed the space and contributed 50 per cent of the cost in return for a mixed-use scheme and increased housing density.

Portlaoise, then called Maryborough, was one of the towns established during the first plantations in Ireland in the 16th century in Laois, formerly known as Queen's County. The remnants of the original fortifications protecting Maryborough are incorporated into the new civic space. The seating and arena arrangement provides an excellent opportunity for outdoor public activities, both formal and informal, and is much used by students from the nearby schools. A new arts and cultural centre within the old Maryborough Port will, when completed, intensify the use of the space. The square is dedicated to James Fitzmaurice who in 1928 was the first person to fly the Atlantic from east to west.

LOCATION on the western edge of the centre of Portlaoise, adjacent to the arts centre
LOCAL AUTHORITY Laois County Council

urban design Shaffrey Associates

WATERFORD: JOHN ROBERTS SQUARE

John Roberts Square is essentially a triangular space at the junction of three traditional shopping streets. It incorporates, refines and extends earlier attempts at traffic calming and establishing pedestrian-priority areas. Waterford is an important city with a history going back to Viking times and the square is situated in the heart of the historic city. Earlier attempts at traffic calming did help somewhat and, in particular, changed the attitudes of the local traders towards pedestrian-priority areas. Because of its location and nature, John Roberts Square is a busy and friendly place. It provides a venue for gatherings and events and is an integral part of Waterford City Council's policy which aims to improve the public spaces within the city and relate them to the introduction of new activities. Collaboration between the architects and artist was very much part of the process with sculpture and public art by Eileen McDonagh.

John Roberts (1714–76) was an important 18th-century Waterford architect. He was responsible for many public buildings including the City Hall and the Church of Ireland and Roman Catholic cathedrals. Incidentally, Waterford has a Le Corbusier Drive and Alvar Aalto Road – they are not architecturally significant.

LOCATION in front of Christchurch Cathedral
LOCAL AUTHORITY Waterford City Council

Architects Department, Waterford City Council

INDEX

A & D Wejchert 10.20
Abercrombie, Patrick 2.3
Aberdeen 9.2, 9.3
Aitcheson, Thomas 1.42
Alec French Partnership **5.6**, **5.8**
Allies and Morrison Architects
    6.10, **7.14**
Alnwick 8.3
Alsop and Störmer **1.34**
Alston 8.3
Andrew Renton and Associates
    1.42
Andrzej Blonski and Michael
    Heard Architects **4.8**
Angus Jamieson Architect **6.16**
Annand, David 9.18
The Architecture and Planning
    Group **5.18**
Armagh, The Market Place **10.4**
Arup Associates **1.4**
Ashbourne 6.3
Atkinson, Fiona 2.4
Aylesbury 4.2

Basildon, Noak Bridge **3.4**
Basildon Development
    Corporation, Architects **3.4**
Bath 5.2
Bauman Lyons Architects **8.4**
BDP **1.20**, **4.4**, **7.32**
Beaumaris 7.3
Belfast 10.3
    Lanyon Place **10.6**
Bentley, J F 1.52
Berwick on Tweed 8.3
Birkenhead, Hamilton Square 7.3
Birmingham 6.2
    Brindleyplace Square 0.7, 6.4,

6.10
Centenary Square **6.8**, 8.28
Chamberlain Square **6.6**
Gas Street Basin 6.4, **6.12**
Victoria Square **6.4**
Birmingham City Council
    Department of Planning and
    Architecture **6.8**
Blaize Hamlet 5.3
Blanchland 8.3
Bolton, Victoria Square **7.4**
Bolton Metropolitan Borough
    Council **7.4**
Borough of Kingston upon Hull
    8.8
Bournemouth 5.2
    The Square **5.4**
Bracknell 4.3
Bradford
    Little Germany 8.2
Bridlington 8.3
    South Promenade **8.4**
Brighton 2.2
    Bartholomew Square 2.6
    beach **2.4**
    Dukes Lane 2.6
    The Lanes **2.6**
Brighton Borough Council **2.4**
Bristol 5.2, 5.3
    Millennium Square **5.8**
    St Augustine's Reach **5.6**
British Waterways Authority
    6.12
Broderick, Cuthbert 8.2, 8.12
Bucklers Hard 4.3
Building Design Partnership **1.20**,
    4.4, **7.32**
Burford 4.2

Burke Kennedy Doyle Architects
    10.22
Burn, William 9.8
Buxton 6.3

CABE 0.10, 1.4
Caernarvon 7.3
Caerphilly 5.3
Calatrava, Santiago 10.12
Calne 5.2
Cambridge, Quayside **3.6**
Camlin Lonsdale Landscape
    Architects **10.6**
Campbell, Robin 5.26
Canterbury 2.3
Canterbury City Council **2.18**
Cardiff, Waterfront **5.10**
Cardiff Bay Development
    Corporation **5.10**
Carlisle 7.2
Carrickfergus 10.3
Cartmel 7.3
CD Partnership **1.26**
Central Manchester Development
    Corporation **7.18**
Ceres 9.2
Chambers, Sir William 1.44
Chapman Taylor Partners 2.12,
    8.32
Chatwin, John **6.10**
Chelmsford, High Street **3.8**
Cheltenham, The Courtyard **5.12**
Chepstow 5.3
Chester, City Centre **7.6**
Chester City Council **7.6**
Chesterfield, Market Square **6.14**
Chesterfield District Council 6.14
Chichester, Pedestrian Area **2.8**

Chorley 7.3
Civic Trust 0.9, 0.10, 0.13
Clayton, John 8.20
Coln Street Community Builders 1.22
Colchester, Culver Square **3.10**
The Commission for Architecture and the Built Environment 0.10, 1.4
Conran Roche **1.18**, **9.24**
Conwy 7.3
Cookham 4.3
Cork Emmet Place **10.8**
Cork City Council **10.8**
Coventry 6.2
Coxwold 8.3
Craig, James 9.2
Crail 9.2
Crawley 2.3, 2.14
Crewe 7.2
Croydon 1.3
Crystal Palace Partnership Programme 1.36
Cullen, Gordon 0.9, 6.2
Culross 9.2
Cumbernauld 9.3
cycle routes 8.16, 10.12
CZWG Architects 1.8, **1.50**

Darbourne and Darke **1.30**
Dawson, Annabelle 1.36
Dent 8.3
Derby 6.2
Derek Latham & Co Architects **8.14**
Derriford 5.24
Derry 10.3
Devizes 5.2

Devon County Council **5.22**, **5.30**
Diamond Lock Grabowski **4.20**
Dixon Jones 0.7, **1.44**, 5.24
Dobson, John 8.20
Donald Insall Associates **1.44**
Donegal, The Diamond **10.10**
Donegal County Council **10.10**
Dorchester, Poundbury **5.14**
Dublin 10.2
  The Campshires **10.12**
  Dublin Castle: Dubh Linn Garden **10.14**
  Meeting House Square **10.18**
  Smithfield **10.20**
  Temple Bar Square **10.16**
Dublin Docklands Development Authority 10.2, **10.12**
Dun Laoghaire
  Ferry Terminal Piazza **10.22**
Dundee 9.2
  High Street 9.4
  Pedestrian Area **9.4**
Durham 8.3
  City Centre **8.6**
Durham City Council **8.6**
Durham County Council **8.6**

Ealing Broadway Centre **1.20**
Ealing Civic Society 1.20
East Ayrshire Council 9.22
East Hertfordshire District Council **3.14**
East Kilbride 9.3
East Sussex County Council **2.12**
Eastbourne 2.3
Eden Project 5.3
Edinburgh 9.2
  Royal Mile **9.6**

The Water of Leith 9.2, **9.8**, 9.24
Ellis Williams Architects 8.18
Elsom Pack & Roberts Partnership **6.14**
English Partnerships 0.10
Eric Lyons, Cunningham and Partners **2.16**
Erik van Egeraat Associated Architects 10.8
Erskine, Ralph **8.16**
Essex County Council **3.16**
Essex Design Guide 3.4, 3.16
Evans & Shalev 5.3
Exeter, Quayside **5.16**
Exeter City Council 5.16

Fakenham, Market Place **3.12**
Fareham, West Street **4.4**
Fareham Borough Council 4.4
Farnham 2.3
  Lion and Lamb Yard **2.10**
Farrell, Terry 9.8
Feilden & Mawson Architects **3.18**, **6.14**
Felixstowe 3.2
Ferguson McIlveen **9.18**
Ferguson Mann Architects **5.6**, **5.8**
Fife 9.2
Finchingfield 3.2
Fitzroy Robinson and Partners **2.6**
Folds, Mark 1.36
Forth Ports plc 9.24
Foster and Partners 8.18, 9.3
Foster John 7.12
Foster, Norman 1.2, 1.3, 1.14, 3.3
Frame, William 5.10
Franklin Ellis Architects **6.20**

INDEX

Franklin Stafford Partnership **7.8**
Frink, Elizabeth 4.18
Frome, The Piggeries **5.18**

Galway 10.3
Garden City movement 3.2
Gateshead 8.3, 8.18
Geddes, Sir Patrick 9.2
Gehl, Jan 6.20
Gibberd, Frederick 3.2
Gifford and Partners 8.18
Gill, Eric 1.52
Gillespies **5.4**, **8.20**, **9.4**, **9.10**,
    9.16
Glasgow 9.3
    Buchanan Street 9.3, **9.10**
    Glasgow Cathedral Precinct
        9.12
    Italian Centre **9.14**
    Royal Exchange Square **9.16**
Glastonbury 5.2
Glenn Howells Architects **10.4**
Glenrothes 9.3
Gloucester, The Docks **5.20**
Gollifer, Andrew 8.26
Gooding, Mel 8.4
Gormley, Anthony 8.3
Gosport 4.3
Gough, Piers 6.10
GRA (Geoffrey Reid Associates)
    4.12
Grafton Architects **10.16**
Grainger Town Partnership 8.20
Grainger, Richard 8.20
Grassington 8.3
Greater London Council 1.42
    Department of Architecture and
        Civic Design **1.6**

Greater London Plan 2.3
Grimshaw, Nicholas 5.3, 5.24
Group 91 Architects **10.16**, **10.18**
Guildford 2.3
Gwynedd County Council 7.24

Haddington 9.2
Halifax, Piece Hall 8.2
Halliday Meecham Partnership
    5.26
Halton Borough Council 7.28
Hamilton, Town Square **9.18**
Hamilton, Thomas 9.8
Hampshire County Architects 4.3
Hampshire County Council **4.18**
Harlow 3.2
Harrison, Thomas 7.3
Harrogate 8.2
Harwich 3.2
Haskoll & Co Ltd Architects **4.16**
Hastings, Town Centre **2.12**
Hastings Borough Council **2.12**
Hatfield 3.2
Hemel Hempstead 3.2
Henley 4.3
Hereford, Left Bank Village **6.16**
Hereford City Council 6.16
Heritage Lottery Fund 1.44
Hertford, Parliament Square **3.14**
Hertfordshire County Council **3.14**
Hexham 8.3
Holder Mathias **3.16**
Hopkins, Michael 1.2, 3.3, 5.8, 6.3
Horsham, Carfax and West Street
    2.14
Horsham District Council **2.14**
The Housing Corporation 0.10
Hove 2.3

Howley Harrington Architects
    10.12
Huddersfield 8.2
Hull, Market Square **8.8**
Hyatt, John 7.20
Hyder Consulting **1.52**

Ian White Associates **9.6**, **9.12**,
    9.22
Inskip & Jenkins **1.44**
International Fund for Ireland
    10.10
Inveraray 9.3
Inverness 9.2
Ipswich 3.2, 3.3
Ironbridge 6.2
Irvine, Harbourside **9.20**
Irvine Development Corporation
    9.20

James and Pearce 3.3
Jaray, Tess 6.8, **8.28**
Jiricna, Eva 1.2
John Dickinson Architect **1.8**, **1.22**
John Dixon Associates **6.20**
John Madin Design Group **6.6**
Johnson, John 3.8
Jon Rowland Urban Design **7.32**
Julyan Wickham and Associates
    1.46

Kaminski, Orla 10.22
Kapoor, Anish **6.22**
Kelly, Michael 10.18
Kelso 9.2
Kemp, David 1.24
Kenda 7.3
Kendrick Associates **4.10**

Kilkenny 10.3
Kilmarnock, Town Centre **9.22**
King's Lynn 3.3, 3.12
Kingston upon Hull, Market
    Square **8.8**
Kinloch, Shona 9.14, 9.22
Kirkby Lonsdale 7.3
Konyn, Geraldine 1.36
Krier, Leon **5.14**

Laganside Corporation 10.3
Lambeth Borough Council 1.22
Lancaster 7.2, 7.3
Landscape Practice Group,
    Birmingham City Council **6.4**
Laois County Council 10.24
Lasdun, Denys 1.32, 3.3
Lavenham 3.2
Leeds 8.2
    The Calls **8.12**, 8.14
    Millennium Square **8.10**
    Victoria Quarter **8.14**
Leicester, Bede Island North **6.18**
Leith, Waterfront **9.24**
Leslie Jones Architects **7.22**
Letchworth 3.2
Leyland 7.3
Libeskind, Daniel 7.30
Lichfield 6.2
lighting 1.36, 1.48, 1.52, 3.12, 4.8,
    4.16, 5.8, 5.10, 8.20, 9.12, 9.16,
    9.18, 10.8, 10.18, 10.20
Limerick 10.2
Lincoln 6.3
Lindisfarne 8.3
Lipton, Stuart 1.4
Liverpool 7.2
    Albert Dock 7.2, **7.8**

Concert Square **7.10**
Derby Square **7.12**
Pier Head **7.14**
Liverpool City Council **7.12**
Livingston 9.3
Llandudno 7.3
Llewelyn-Davies **7.32**, **8.12**
Lomax, Tom 6.8
London
    Broadgate 0.7, 1.2, **1.4**
    Camden Lock **1.8**
    Chinatown: Gerrard Street **1.10**
    Comyn Ching Triangle **1.12**
    Covent Garden **1.6**
    Docklands 1.42
        Canary Wharf **1.14**
        Crossharbour **1.16**
        Greenland Dock **1.18**
    Ealing Broadway Centre **1.20**
    Gabriel's Wharf **1.22**
    Hay's Galleria **1.24**
    Horselydown Square **1.46**
    King's Road, Bluebird **1.26**
    Leicester Square 1.2, **1.28**
    Lillington Street **1.30**
    National Theatre 1.22
        Theatre Square **1.32**
    Peckham, Town Square **1.34**
    Penge High Street **1.36**
    Richmond Riverside **1.38**
    St Christopher's Place **1.40**
    St Katherine's Dock **1.42**
    Somerset House **1.44**
    Tower Bridge Piazza 0.7, **1.46**
    Wandsworth, Battersea Square
        1.48
    Westbourne Grove **1.50**
    Westminster Cathedral Piazza

1.52
London Docklands Development
    Corporation **1.16**, 1.42
Londonderry 10.3
Ludlow 6.2
Lymington 4.3
Lyons+Sleeman+Hoare Architects
    2.10

MacCormac Jamieson Prichard 1.2
McLean, Bruce **8.4**
Maidenhead 4.3
Malcolm Fraser Architects 9.8
Maldon 3.3
Manchester 0.7, 7.2
    Albert Square 7.2, **7.16**
    Castlefield 0.7, 7.2, **7.18**
    Exchange Square **7.20**
    Great Northern Square **7.22**
Manchester City Council **7.16**
Market Harborough 6.2
Marks Barfield Architects 7.8
Marlborough 5.2
Marlow 4.3
Marsh and Grochowski Architects
    6.22
Marsh Mills 5.24
Martin, Leslie 4.2
Mason, Raymond 6.8
Matcham, Frank 8.14
Mather, Rick 1.32, 3.3
MBM 9.10
McDonagh, Eileen 10.26
McGarry Ni Eanaigh Architects
    10.20
Mendip District Council 5.18
Michael Wilford & Associates
    7.30

INDEX

Milton Keynes 4.2
   Queen's Square **4.6**
   Theatre Square **4.8**
Milton Keynes Development
   Corporation **4.6**
Mitchell & Associates **10.22**
Monmouth 5.3
Moro, Peter 6.3, 6.22
Mousehole 5.2

Nash, John 5.3
National Trust for Scotland 9.2
New Ash Green 2.3, **2.16**
New Lanark 9.3
new towns 0.9, 2.3, 2.14, 3.2,
   3.14, 4.3, 7.3, 7.28, 8.3, 9.3
New Towns Act 9.20
Newbury 4.3
Newcastle upon Tyne 8.3
   Byker **8.16**
   East Quayside **8.18**
   Grainger Town **8.20**
Newton Abbot 5.22
   Courtenay Street **5.22**
Newton Aycliffe 8.3
Nicholas Hare Architects **5.10**
Nicholas Ray Associates **3.6**
North Ayrshire District Council
   9.20
North Norfolk District Council
   3.12
Norwich, Elm Hill **3.18**
Nottingham 6.2, 6.3
   Castle Wharf **6.20**
   Playhouse Square **6.22**
   Sky Mirror 6.22

O'Connell, Eilís 5.6

O'Doherty, Eamon 10.22
O'Donnell and Tuomey 10.18
O'Toole, Shane 10.18
Office of Public Works **10.14**
Oxford, Gloucester Green **4.10**
Oxford City Council 4.10

Page & Park Architects **9.6**, **9.12**,
   9.14, **9.22**
Panter Hudspith Architects **8.30**
Paoletti, Roland 1.2
Paolozzi, Eduardo 9.8
parking 5.14, 7.28, 8.16, 10.10
Pasmore, Victor 8.3
Paul Keogh Architects **10.18**
paving 1.18, 1.34, 1.36, 1.48, 1.52,
   4.18, 5.28, 6.8, 6.18, 7.16, 8.6,
   8.8, 8.20, 8.22, 8.28, 8.30, 9.6,
   9.16, 9.18, 10.8, 10.10, 10.12,
   10.20
Paxton, Joseph 7.3
Peckham, Town Square **1.34**
pedestrian areas 1.4, 1.6, 2.8,
   2.12, 3.14, 4.4, 4.16, 4.18, 4.20,
   5.4, 6.4, 6.18, 7.4, 7.8, 7.16,
   7.20, 7.26, 7.32, 7.34, 8.6, 8.16,
   8.20, 8.28, 8.30, 8.32, 9.3, 9.4,
   9.10, 9.12, 9.18, 9.22, 10.4, 10.8,
   10.10, 10.26
pedestrian-priority areas 5.30,
   9.16
Pelli, Cesar 1.14
Penge 1.3
   High Street **1.36**
Perth 9.2
Peterlee 8.3
Philip Cave Associates **1.36**
Phillips, Niall **5.16**

planning gain 10.24
planting 1.32, 5.4, 5.22, 9.12
Plymouth, The Barbican **5.24**
Plymouth City Council **5.24**
Polperro 5.2
Poole 5.3
Porphyrios, Demetri 6.10
Port Sunlight 7.3
Portlaoise
   Fitzmaurice Place **10.24**
Portmeirion 7.3, **7.24**
Portsmouth 4.3
   Gun Wharf Quays **4.12**, 4.14
   Old Town **4.14**
Portsmouth City Council **4.14**
Poundbury 5.2, **5.14**
Powell and Moya 1.30
Preston, Market Square **7.26**
Preston Borough Council **7.26**
public art 1.4, 2.4, 2.10, 3.12, 4.4,
   5.26, 5.30, 6.8, 7.32, 8.3, 8.8,
   8.10, 8.20, 8.24, 9.4, 9.14, 9.16,
   9.18, 9.22, 10.12, 10.22, 10.26
Pye, William 1.40, 5.8

Quinlan Terry Associates **1.38**

Reading, Oracle Centre **4.16**
Rennie, Sir John 10.22
RHWL 7.22
Rhyl 7.3
Richard Hemingway Architects
   6.16
Richard Rogers Partnership 1.4,
   1.26
Richborough Castle 2.2
Richman, Martin 5.8
Richmond (Yorkshire) 8.3

Richmond on Thames, Riverside **1.38**
Ripon 8.2
Roberts, John 10.26
Robinson & McIlwaine Architects 10.6
Rochester 2.2
Rotherham, Magna Centre 8.2
Royal Borough of Kensington and Chelsea 1.26, 1.50
Royal Borough of Windsor and Maidenhead 4.20
Royal Fine Arts Commission 0.10
Royal Leamington Spa 6.2
RTKL Architects **7.30**
Runcorn 7.3, 7.28
    Halton Brow **7.28**
Runcorn Development Corporation **7.28**
Rye 2.2

Saarinen, Eero 1.40
Saffron Walden 3.2
St Austell 5.3
St Ives 5.3
Salford, The Lowry Plaza **7.30**
Salisbury 5.2
Salt, Titus 8.2
Saltaire 8.2
Sandwich 2.2
Scarborough 8.3
Schwartz, Martha **7.20**
Scott, Michael 10.8
Scottish Development Agency 9.24
Serra, Richard 1.4
Sevenoaks District Council 2.16
Shaffrey Associates **10.24**

Sharp, Thomas 4.2
Sheffield 8.2
    Peace Gardens **8.22**
    Victoria Quays **8.24**
Sheffield Design and Property **8.22**
Sheffield Urban Development Corporation **8.24**
Shepheard, Epstein and Hunter 7.30
Sheppard Robson **3.10**
Short Ford Associates 6.3
Sidell Gibson 6.10
Sitte, Camillo 6.10
Skelmersdale New Town 7.3
Skidmore Owings and Merrill **1.14, 7.22**
Sloan, Jack 9.12, 9.14
Snowdonia National Park 7.24
Soane, Sir John 1.4
SOM **1.14, 7.22**
South Lanarkshire District Council 9.18
South Woodham Ferrers 3.2, 3.16
    Town Centre **3.16**
Southampton 4.3
Southwark Building Design Services **1.34**
Span (Developments) Ltd 2.16
Staindrop 8.3
Stamford 6.3
Stanley Partnership Architects **5.12, 5.20**
Stanton Williams Associates **1.32,** 6.10
Stevenage 3.2
Stirling, James 6.3
Stock Woolstencroft 1.36

Stockley Park 1.3
Stoddart, Sandy 9.14
Stokes, Leonard 4.10
Stowe 4.2
Stratford upon Avon 6.2
street furniture 1.10, 2.4, 3.8, 3.12, 3.14, 5.28, 6.18, 7.4, 8.20, 9.4, 9.6, 9.12, 9.16, 9.22, 10.8
Sunderland, St Peter's Riverside **8.26**
Sunderland City Council 8.26
Swansea 5.3
    Maritime Quarter **5.26**
    Wind Street **5.28**
Swansea City Council **5.26, 5.28**

Teignbridge District Council 5.22, **5.30**
Teignmouth, The Triangles **5.30**
Telford 6.2
Telford, Thomas 9.8
Temple Bar Square **10.16**
Terry Farrell & Partners **1.12, 8.18**
Terry Farrell Partnership **6.10**
Thaxted 3.2
Thorp, John **8.10**
Tibbalds, Francis 0.9
Totnes 5.3
Townshend Landscape Architects **1.40**
traffic calming 3.6, 5.14, 10.26
tree planting 1.36, 1.48, 3.8, 3.14, 4.10, 4.16, 5.28, 6.10, 7.22, 8.8, 8.28, 9.12, 10.8, 10.12
Trinity Architects **5.4**
Tunbridge Wells 2.3
Twigg Brown and Partners **1.24**

INDEX

Tyne and Wear Urban
    Development Corporation **8.26**

University of Sunderland 8.26
Urban Design Alliance 0.10
Urban Design Group 0.6, 0.9,
    0.10, 0.11
Urban Design Group, Leicester
    City Council **6.18**
Urban Initiatives 10.8
Urban Splash **7.10**
URBED **5.16**, 5.28

Wakefield
    Kirkgate **8.28**
Wakefield City Council **8.28**
Walker, Derek 4.6
Walsall 6.2
Wandsworth, Battersea Square
    1.48
Wandsworth Borough Council
    1.48
Ward, David 5.8
Warkworth 8.3
Warrington 7.3
Warwick 6.2
Washington 8.3
water 1.18, 1.42, 1.44, 1.48, 2.14,
    3.10, 4.12, 5.6, 5.8, 5.10, 5.26,
    6.4, 6.10, 6.12, 6.22, 7.22, 8.10,
    8.22, 8.24, 9.14
Waterford 10.3
    John Roberts Square **10.26**
Waterford City Council **10.26**
Waterhouse, Alfred 7.16
Watkinson, Simon **3.12**
Waverley Borough Council 2.10
Wells 5.2

Welwyn Garden City 3.2
West Dorset District Council 5.14
West Sussex County Council **2.8**
Westminster City Council 1.6,
    1.10, 1.12, **1.28**, 1.40, 1.44, 1.52
Westport 10.3
Wexford 10.2
Weymouth 5.3
Whitehaven, Waterfront **7.32**
Whitfield, William 6.16
Whitstable, Fishermen's Buildings
    2.18
Wigan, Market Place **7.34**
Wigan Borough Council **7.34**
Wilkinson Eyre 5.8, 8.2, 8.18
Williams-Ellis, Clough **7.24**
Winchelsea 2.2
Winchester 2.3, 4.2, 4.3
    County Records Office 4.18
    High Street **4.18**
    Walcote Place 4.18
Winchester City Council 4.18
Windsor 4.2
    Central Station **4.20**
Witney 4.2
Woburn 4.2
Wolverhampton 6.2
Wood the Elder, John 5.2
Wood the Younger, John 5.2
Woodstock 4.2
Worthing 2.3
Worthington, Thomas 7.16
Worthington, John 0.6
Wyatt, James 7.12, 10.3

York 8.2
    Riverside **8.30**
    St Mary's Square **8.32**

Picture Credits
Photographs by John Billingham
    and Richard Cole, except:
1.4 Arup Associates
1.26 Morley von Sternberg
1.36 Philip Cave
1.50 Keith Collie
2.18 Derek Abbott
3.14 East Hertfordshire District
    Council
3.16 Alan Stones
3.18 Gerald Dix
5.10 Louis Poulsen
7.34 Craig Photography
8.4 Martin Peters
8.18 Keith Hunter
8.22 Sheffield Design & Property
9.4 Dundee City Council
9.8 Sarah Collings
9.14 Page & Park Architects
9.22 Civic Trust Awards 1997
10.6 Rajesh Rana
10.10 Megannety Photography
10.24 Laois County Council
10.26 Michelle Brett

Front cover: Sheffield Design &
    Property